INSOLVENCY
Procedure Notes (2nd Edi

G000134787

PAUL GORDON-SAKER,
Solicitor, Alsop Wilkinson
MICHAEL STUBBS, B.Sc. (Econ.)
Solicitor, Alsop Wilkinson

WATERLOW PUBLISHERS

Second edition 1991
© Waterlow Publishers 1987, 1991

Waterlow Publishers
50 Fetter Lane
London EC4A 1AA
A division of Pergamon Press PLC

ISBN 0 08 036917 0

British Library Cataloguing in Publication Data

Gordon-Saker, Paul
    Insolvency: procedure notes.—(WPL).
    1. England. Insolvency. Law. Procedure
    I. Title II. Stubbs, Michael, 1955—
    344.206'78'0269

Printed in Great Britain by BPCC Wheatons Ltd, Exeter

Preface

The purpose of this book is to provide a concise guide to the more frequently used procedures to be followed in cases of corporate and personal insolvency. The Insolvency Act 1986 and the Insolvency Rules 1986 came into force on 29 December 1986 and provide a statutory code of practice. Appointments as receiver under the Law of Property Act 1925 and the Agricultural Credits Act 1928 remain outside the provisions of this new code. Those appointments apart, only a person qualified to act as an insolvency practitioner may now take appointments in relation to companies as:

> liquidator
> provisional liquidator
> administrator
> administrative receiver, or
> supervisor of a voluntary arrangement

and in relation to individuals as:

> trustee in bankruptcy
> trustee under a deed of arrangement
> supervisor of a voluntary arrangement, or
> in certain circumstances, as administrator of an insolvent estate of a deceased individual

By s.389(1) of the Insolvency Act 1986 a person who acts as an insolvency practitioner whilst unqualified is liable on conviction to imprisonment or to a fine or both. The official receiver alone is excluded.

Certain recognised professional bodies are authorised by the Secretary of State to grant or refuse applications from their members for authorisation to act as an insolvency practitioner. These bodies include the Institute of Chartered Accountants for England and Wales, the Insolvency Practitioners Association, the Chartered Association of Certified Accountants and the Law Society. A person who is not a member of an authorised professional body must apply to the Secretary of State. The different professional bodies have imposed differing standards in assessing applicants. All however require proof of experience. Examinations are to be introduced in 1990.

It is hoped that this guide will be of practical use to insolvency practitioners and their staffs, to solicitors and accountants generally and also to debtors and creditors, all of whom are faced with new procedures, new principles and new law. It is not intended that this guide be used as a substitute for the Insolvency Act 1986 and the Insolvency Rules 1986. But we hope it will be a useful introduction to those areas of the law referred to and a concise reference, or checklist, to the more commonly used procedures. No attempt is made to interpret the law and in that regard the reader is referred to the various annotated statutes already published.

The law as stated is that which applies to England and Wales as at 31 May 1990. In the three years since the first edition there have been a number of amendments to the Rules, the effect of some of which has been to make material changes to the procedures introduced in 1986.

Except where the context dictates otherwise, references to forms and rules are references to the forms and rules in the Insolvency Rules 1986 (SI 1986 No 1925) as amended by the Insolvency (Amendment) Rules 1987 (SI 1987 No 1919). Statutory references are to the Insolvency Act 1986.

AUTHOR'S NOTE

To assist those who wish to refer to the original texts of the rules and amendments, where amended rules are referred to they are marked * and the references to forms are shown as either "new" or "amended" as appropriate.

Contents

Table of Forms

Table of Rules

Table of Statutes

Insolvency Act 1986 *cont.*

1. Company Voluntary Arrangements

Contents *page*

1.0 Introduction

Voluntary arrangements for companies are a procedure to enable a company to conclude an effective arrangement with its creditors. Those proposing the arrangement appoint a nominee (who must be an insolvency practitioner) to report to the court and to summon meetings of creditors and contributories. If 75 per cent in value of the creditors agree, the arrangement becomes binding on all persons who had notice of the meeting and were entitled to vote at it. A supervisor is appointed to oversee the arrangement. The supervisor may be the nominee or another insolvency practitioner.

1.1 Proposal

By directors

1.1.1 Directors prepare proposal for intended nominee to report to the court. Must contain:

    (1) explanation why in directors' opinion a voluntary arrangement is desirable and why creditors should agree
    (2) statement of company's assets with values
    (3) details of charges on assets
    (4) the extent, if any, to which particular assets are to be excluded
    (5) details of any property not owned by the company which is to be included
    (6) details of liablilites and how they are to be met or otherwise dealt with, referring specifically to:
        (a) preferential and secured creditors
        (b) treatment of any creditors connected with the company
        (c) knowledge by directors of possible claims in the event of liquidation under ss.238 (transactions at an undervalue), 239 (preferences), 244 (extortionate credit transactions), 245 (invalid floating charges) and details of how, if at all, company is to be indemnified in respect of such claims.
    (7) details of guarantees
    (8) proposed duration of arrangement
    (9) proposed distributions (dates and amounts)
    (10) proposed remuneration of nominee and supervisor
    (11) details of any guarantees or security to be given for arrangement
    (12) proposals as to investment and banking of funds
    (13) details of how funds unpaid to creditors on termination of the arrangement are to be dealt with
    (14) proposals as to conduct of business of company
    (15) details of any further credit applications and their repayment
    (16) details of functions of supervisor
    (17) name address and qualification of proposed supervisor
s.1
rr. 1.2, 1.3   [No prescribed form]

1.1.2 With the written agreement of the nominee the proposal may be amended at any time up to delivery to the court of the nominee's report.
rr. 1.2, 1.3   [No prescribed form]

1.2   Nominee

1.2.1 Directors give notice of proposal to nominee, in writing with copy of proposal.
r. 1.4(1)   [No prescribed form]

1.2.2 Nominee agreeing to act endorses copy notice with date of receipt and returns copy notice to directors.
s. 2
r. 1.4(3) and (4)   [No prescribed form]

3 Statement of affairs

3.1 Within 7 days of delivery of proposal to nominee (or within such extended time as he may allow) directors shall deliver to nominee a statement of the company's affairs which must comprise:
(1) list of assets with values
(2) particulars of secured claims
(3) names and addresses of and amounts due to preferential creditors
(4) names and addresses of and amounts due to unsecured creditors
(5) particulars of debts due to or from persons connected with the company
(6) names and addresses of company's members and details of shareholdings
(7) such other particulars as the nominee may in writing require to be furnished for the purposes of making his report
rr. 1.5, 1.6 [No prescribed form]

3.2 Statement of affairs must not be made up to date earlier than 2 weeks before date of notice to nominee. The nominee may extend period but must give reasons. Two or more officers of company must certify statement as correct. Nominee may call for further information. Directors must give nominee access to records of company.
rr. 1.5, 1.6

4 Nominee's report

4.1 Nominee must report to court within 28 days of date of return of notice of agreement to act or must apply to court for extension. Report must state:
(1) if nominee considers meetings of company and creditors should be summoned, and
(2) date time and place of such meetings, and
(3) if meetings are to be summoned, the nominee's comments on the directors' proposal, or
(4) nominee's reasons for not requesting meetings
s. 2 [No prescribed form]

4.2 Nominee must deliver to court with report:
(1) copy of directors' proposal (with any authorised amendments)
(2) copy or summary of statement of affairs
r. 1.7(1)

4.3 Court dates nominee's report. Any director, member or creditor may inspect.
r. 1.7(3)

1.4.4   Nominee sends copy report to company.
         r. 1.7(4)

1.4.5   If nominee fails to report on time a director may apply for his
         replacement to the court on 7 days' notice.
         s. 2
         r. 1.8   [No prescribed form]

1.5   Summoning of meetings

1.5.1   Where nominee has reported that meetings of members and credi-
         tors should be summoned nominee proceeds to summon meetings to
         be held as proposed in report not less than 14 nor more than 28 days
         from filing a report with court.
         s. 3
         r. 1.9   [No prescribed form]

1.5.2   Nominee gives creditors and members 14 days' notice of their
         respective meetings. Notices must specify court to which nominee's
         report delivered and state effect of rule on majority voting. With
         each notice must be sent:
         (1) copy directors' proposal
         (2) copy statement of affairs (or summary)
         (3) nominee's comments on proposal
         s. 3
         r. 1.9   [No prescribed form]

1.6   Other proposals

1.6.1   Administrator or liquidator may make proposal with himself as
         nominee containing same detail as directors' proposal plus any
         additional matters as may be appropriate to enable members and
         creditors to reach an informed decision. Where the company is
         subject to an administration order this proposal must include the
         names and addresses of the preferential creditors with the amount
         due to each of them.
         s. 1
         r. 1.10*   [No prescribed form]

1.6.2   Notices of meetings given to members and creditors at least 14 days
         before, and including copy proposal and statement of affairs or
         summary.
         r. 1.11   [No prescribed form]

1.6.3 Forms of proxy to be sent out with notices.
[form 8.1]

1.6.4 Administrator or liquidator with notices of meetings may propose another nominee in which case he must give notice to nominee and prepare proposal as by directors (1.1.1 above) and provide with it a copy of the company's statement of affairs and if in administration details of the preferential creditors (1.6.1 above).
r. 1.12* [No prescribed form]

1.6.5 Where company is being wound up by the court the official receiver is sent a copy of the proposal and details of nominee.
r. 1.12 [No prescribed form]

1.7 Procedure at meetings

1.7.1 Person summoning meeting is called convenor. In fixing venue he shall have regard first to convenience of creditors. Meetings must be between 10 am and 4 pm on a business day. Creditors' and company meetings to be on same day at same place but creditors' meeting first.
s. 3
r. 1.13

1.7.2 Convenor acts as meeting chairman but if unable to attend another insolvency practitioner may do so or an employee of the convenor or his firm who has insolvency experience.
r. 1.14

1.7.3 Chairman may not vote his proxies on questions of remuneration unless specifically directed.
r. 1.15

1.7.4 At least 14 days' notice must be given by convenor to directors and also to former officers if convenor thinks fit.
r. 1.16(1) [No prescribed form]

1.7.5 Chairman may exclude any present director or former officer from meeting even if notified to attend.
r. 1.16(2)

1.7.6 Every creditor given notice of meeting may vote. To pass the proposal or a modification of it requires a majority in excess of 75 per cent in value of creditors present and voting in person or by proxy. In respect of any other resolution majority must exceed 50 per cent in value.
rr. 1.17, 1.19

1.7.7 Members vote according to the rights attaching to their shares but a
       member with no such voting rights may vote for or against the
       proposal but without affecting the result. Majority is more than 50
       per cent in value of members voting in person or by proxy. Value of
       members' votes is determined by reference to the company's
       articles.
       rr. 1.18, 1.20*

1.7.8 If requisite majority for approval of the arrangement is not obtained
       from both creditors and members, chairman may, if so resolved,
       adjourn meetings if resolutions passed to that effect. Nominee must
       notify court of adjournment.
       r. 1.21

1.7.9 Adjourned meetings of creditors and members must be on the same
       day and within 14 days of original meeting. If proposal not then
       agreed it is rejected.
       r. 1.21

1.7.10 Chairman reports result to court within 4 days.
       s. 4

1.8   Challenge of decisions

1.8.1 Application may be made to court by either:
       (1) creditor or member
       (2) nominee
       (3) liquidator
       (4) administrator
       alleging either or both:
       (a) decision of meeting unfairly prejudices creditor, member or
            contributory
       (b) a material irregularity at or in relation to either of the meetings
       s. 6

1.8.2 Application must be made within 28 days of chairman's report to
       court of result of meetings.
       s. 6(3)

1.8.3 Court may:
       (1) revoke or suspend approvals given by meetings
       (2) direct summoning of further meetings to consider revised
            proposal
       (3) dismiss the application
       s. 6(4)

1.8.4   If court suspends or revokes approvals, person applying for order serves sealed copies on supervisor and persons making proposal and, within 7 days, on registrar of companies. (Service on directors is by service of single copy of order on the company at its registered office.)
r. 1.25   [form 1.2]

1.8.5   If order includes direction for further meetings notice of the order is given to person required by it to summon meetings.
r. 1.25(3)

1.8.6   Persons making proposal forthwith give notice of order to all persons notified of meetings or who may be affected by order and within 7 days notify court whether they intend to make revised proposal or invite reconsideration of original proposal.
s. 6
r. 1.25(4)

1.9   Implementation of proposal

1.9.1   If voluntary arrangement is approved by meetings the directors (or the liquidator or administrator) hand over property of company to the person appointed as supervisor of the arrangement.
ss. 5, 7
r. 1.23

1.9.2   Supervisor sends copy of chairman's report to registrar of companies.
r. 1.24   [amended form 1.1]

1.9.3   If supervisor is to carry on business, or realise assets or administer funds he is required to keep accounts.
r. 1.26   [No prescribed form]

1.9.4   At least every 12 months supervisor must prepare receipts and payments account with progress report and send to:
(1)   the court
(2)   the registrar of companies
(3)   the company
(4)   all creditors bound by the arrangement
(5)   members bound by the arrangement
(6)   auditors of the company if it is not in liquidation
r. 1.26   [form 1.3]

1.9.5   Secretary of State has power at any time to require supervisor to
         produce records accounts and reports either at supervisor's premises
         or elsewhere.
         r. 1.27

1.10   Completion of the arrangement

1.10.1   Within 28 days of final completion supervisor gives notice of such
         to all creditors and members and with it a report detailing all
         receipts and payments and explaining any differences between actual
         implementation and proposal.
         r. 1.29(1) and (2)

1.10.2   Copies of notice and report sent by supervisor to court and registrar
         of companies.
         r. 1.29(3)   [form 1.4]

1.10.3   Court may extend 28 day period.
         r. 1.29(4)

2. Administration Orders

Contents *page*

2.0 Introduction

Administration was an entirely new procedure recommended in the Cork Report, the purpose of which is to rescue and rehabilitate an actually or potentially insolvent company as to the whole or part of its undertaking. Failing that (or alternatively), to effect a more advantageous realisation of the company's assets than would be the case on immediate winding up. The wide powers of the administrator, as set out in Part II of the Act, are analogous to those of the administrative receiver set out in Chapter I of Part III of the Act. The success or otherwise of the procedure will largely depend upon the skill, imagination and resources of the administrator; the acquiescence of the bank (having power to appoint an administrative receiver under a floating charge); and its application in appropriate circumstances. In view of the necessary complexity of the rules it is unlikely to be a practical option in the case of very small companies.

From the time an administration order is applied for until the dismissal of the petition or, if an order is made, until its discharge, there is in effect a general moratorium of the company's affairs during which time:

(1)   the company cannot be wound up
(2)   no steps may be taken to enforce any security or repossess goods (including goods on hire purchase, lease, or subject to retention of title claims)
(3)   no proceedings or execution may be commenced or continued except with the consent of administrator or leave of court

Further, when an order is made all other insolvency procedures are inapplicable for its duration, and any receiver appointed must vacate office.

The administrator is deemed to be the agent of the company (s. 14) and acts without personal liability. In those circumstances it remains to be seen whether he will be able to arrange finance if necessary and whether, or on what terms, suppliers and customers will be prepared to deal with the company.

2.1   Application for an order

2.1.1   Applicant may be the company, its directors (but not a director unless he is also a creditor), a creditor or creditors (including contingent or prospective) or any combination thereof.
s. 9(1)

2.1.2   Order will not be made if company already in liquidation (or if company is an insurance company) or if person who appointed an existing administrative receiver does not positively consent (unless that security liable to release, avoidance or challenge).
ss. 8(4), 9(2) and (3)

2.1.3   Application to the court having jurisdiction to wind up the company (see 4.1 below) by petition with affidavit in support. Once presented, petition cannot be withdrawn except with leave of court.
s. 9(2)
amended form 2.1   [No prescribed form of affidavit]

2.1.4   Notice of the presented petition must be given forthwith to any person who has appointed or is entitled to appoint an administrative receiver (debenture holder).
s. 9(2)

2.1.5 The court's power to make order is permissive not mandatory if conditions are satisfied. Otherwise it may dismiss, adjourn, make interim order or any other order.
s. 8(1)

2.2 Petition

2.2.1 Petition by company or directors must state name of company and address for service (usually registered office).
r. 2.4(1)

2.2.2 Petition by single creditor must state his name and address for service. Petition by more than one creditor must name all such creditors but give address for service of one creditor who, after presentation, will be treated as principal.
r. 2.4(2) and (4)

2.2.3 Any petition must specify name and address of proposed administrator and state (to best of petitioner's knowledge and belief) that person is qualified to act as insolvency practitioner in relation to the company.
rr. 2.4 (5) and (6)   [amended form 2.1]

2.3 Affidavit in support

2.3.1 If petition by company or directors, affidavit must be made by a director or secretary stating it is made on behalf of company or directors. If petition by creditor(s), affidavit must be made by person acting under the authority of all of them, stating nature of authority and means of knowledge.
r. 2.3   [No prescribed form of affidavit]

2.3.2 Affidavit must state:
(1) deponent's belief that company is, or is likely to become, unable to pay its debts, and grounds for belief
(2) which specified purpose it is expected will be achieved by making order ie:
  (a) survival of company, and whole or part of its undertaking, as a going concern
  (b) approval of voluntary arrangement under Part I of the Act
  (c) sanctioning of a compromise or arrangement (Companies Act 1985, s. 425)
  (d) more advantageous realisation of company's assets than if wound up
s. 8(3)
r. 2.3

2.3.3   Affidavit must also include (to best of deponent's knowledge and belief):
(1)   statement of company's financial position specifying assets and liabilities including contingent and prospective
(2)   details of any security held by creditors and any power to appoint an administrative receiver (and stating if receiver is appointed)
(3)   details of any presented petition to wind up company
(4)   any other matters which may assist the court
(5)   statement that independent report has been prepared (or if not, why not)
r. 2.3 (2)-(6)

2.3.4   Exhibits to affidavit:
(1)   copy of petition
(2)   written consent to act of proposed administrator
(3)   evidence of positive consent of any person who has appointed an administrative receiver (if already obtained)
(4)   copy of independent report if prepared
r. 2.4(6)   [form 2.2]

2.3.5   An independent report may be prepared, by a person not involved in the company but having adequate knowledge of the company's affairs (may be the proposed administrator) showing why appointment of administrator expedient. Not mandatory but obviously persuasive.
r. 2.2   [No prescribed form]

2.4   Filing and service of petition

2.4.1   File petition and affidavit with court (with service copies and one extra). Court seals and notes venue for hearing on each copy petition. Petitioner must notify court in writing of any subsequently presented winding up petition.
rr. 2.5, 2.6

2.4.2   Copy of sealed petition, affidavit and any exhibits (other than petition) must be served on:
(1)   any person who has appointed administrative receiver, or is or may be entitled to do so
(2)   administrative receiver (if appointed)
(3)   a petitioner of a pending winding-up petition

(4) proposed administrator
(5) the company (if creditors' petition)
s. 9(2)
r. 2.6*

2.4.3 Forthwith, after filing petition, notice of its presentation must be given to any sheriff or other officer levying execution or other process against company, and any person who has distrained.
r. 2.6A*

2.4.4 Personal or postal (first class) service by petitioner, his solicitor or agent of either, delivery being not less than 5 days before date of hearing. Serve on company at its registered office (or, if not practicable, at last known principal place of business); or on any other person at his proper or last known address; or otherwise as court may direct. In the case of a bank or other or former authorised institution under the Banking Act 1987 which has not notified an address for service, the petition should be served at the address where the company maintains a bank account.
r. 2.7*

2.4.5 Affidavit verifying service (date, manner, address) exhibiting sealed copy of petition must be filed not less than one day before hearing.
r. 2.8   [form 2.3]

2.5 The hearing

2.5.1 Any of the following may appear or be represented at hearing of petition:
(1) petitioner
(2) company
(3) any person who has appointed administrative receiver, or is or may be entitled to appoint one
(4) administrative receiver (if appointed)
(5) any person who has presented winding-up petition
(6) proposed administrator
(7) any other interested person with leave of court
r. 2.9 (1)*

2.5.2 If order is made, costs of petitioner (and other persons appearing if court allows) are payable in the administration.
r. 2.9 (2)   [form 2.4]

2.6 Notice and advertisement of order

2.6.1 Upon order, administrator must advertise forthwith:
(1) once in the Gazette
(2) once in newspaper most appropriate to creditors
r. 2.10 (2)   [amended form 2.5]

2.6.2 Administrator must also give notice of order, forthwith, to:
(1) any person who has appointed administrative receiver, or is or may be entitled to appoint one
(2) administrative receiver (if appointed)
(3) petitioner of any pending winding-up petition (or provisional liquidator)
(4) registrar of companies (sealed copy)
r. 2.10 (3) and (4)   [forms 2.6, 2.7]

2.7 Statement of affairs

2.7.1 Administrator must forthwith procure the preparation of a statement of affairs, by some or all of:
(1) present or past officers of the company
(2) those who have taken part at any time within the past year in the formation of the company
(3) present or past employees (within one year previous)
(4) present of past officers or employees of another company which is or was within one year, an officer of the company
(Such persons are referred to in Chapter 2 of the Rules as 'deponents'.)
s. 22
r. 2.11*   [form 2.9]

2.7.2 Statement will include particulars of company's assets, debts and liabilities, names and addresses of creditors, securities held by creditors and the dates when securities were given.
s. 22 (2)

2.7.3 Administrator sends notice to such deponents as he considers appropriate, requiring them to submit statement. The notice must inform each deponent of:
(1) details of other deponents to whom notice sent
(2) time limit for delivery of statement
(3) deponent's legal duty to provide information, and penalty for non-compliance
s. 235
r. 2.11*   [amended form 2.8]

2.7.4 Deponent must verify statement of affairs by affidavit (included in form 2.9) and administrator may require any other potential deponent to submit affidavit of concurrence (which may be qualified). Administrator then files copy of verified statement (and any affidavits of concurrence) with court.
r. 2.12

2.7.5 If administrator thinks that disclosure of whole or part of statement of affairs may prejudice administration he may apply to court for order of limited disclosure.
r. 2.13

2.7.6 Administrator may release deponent from obligation or deponent may apply to court, usually at his own cost.
s. 22(5)
r. 2.14

2.7.7 Deponent's reasonable expenses in making statement of affairs will be expenses in the administration.
r. 2.15

2.8 Proposals to creditors

2.8.1 Within 3 months of order administrator formulates statement of proposals for achieving purpose(s) specified in order, and sends to:
(1) registrar of companies
(2) all creditors (of whom he is aware)
(3) all members (or offers to in advertisement) and calls meeting of creditors on 14 days' notice. In default administrator is liable to fine.
s. 23   [No prescribed form]

2.8.2 Administrator must annex statement to proposals when sent to registrar of companies and laid before creditors' meetings including:
(1) details of appointment, purpose or order on application and any subsequent variation
(2) circumstances of application
(3) names of directors and secretary
(4) statement of affairs, or summary, with comments or recent financial details if no statement of affairs
(5) give details of management and finance of company since administrator's appointment; and
(6) proposals for future management and finance of company
r. 2.16*   [No prescribed form]

2.8.3 Where administrator intends to apply to court for discharge of order before he has sent proposals to creditors, he must send creditors report of matters 2.8.2(1)–(5) at least 10 days before application to discharge.
ss. 18, 23
r. 2.16*

2.8.4 Notice of proposals to creditors is given to members by advertising in the Gazette and once in newspaper in which order was advertised.
r. 2.17

2.9   Creditors' meeting

2.9.1   Creditors' meeting decides whether to approve administrator's proposals which may be modified if administrator consents. If proposal rejected, administrator reports to court (and registrar of companies which may discharge order, or make other order. If proposal approved, administrator manages company's business and property accordingly.
s. 24

2.9.2   Twenty-one days' notice of meeting with proxy form to be given to all known creditors, and advertised in same newspaper as order advertised, and notice to attend meeting to be sent to present or past directors and officers as required (except as to meetings under ss. 23(1) and 25(2) where 14 days' notice of meeting is required).
rr. 2.18, 2.19*   [forms 2.10, amended 2.11, 8.2]

2.9.3   Meeting to be held between 10 am and 4 pm on business day at venue convenient to creditors. If no chairman present, adjourn 7 days. Chairman may adjourn for maximum 14 days. Chairman is administrator or nominee being an experienced colleague.
    Above rules apply to all creditors' meetings in administration.
r. 2.19

2.9.4   Creditor(s) of 10 per cent in value can at any time request (giving reasons) administrator to summon creditors' meeting and such meeting to be within 35 days. Such meeting may be at that creditor's expense (unless meeting otherwise resolves) and he must first deposit appropriate sum with administrator.
s. 17
r. 2.21

2.9.5   Creditor may vote only if: he gives written details of debt (and proxy form if appropriate) to administrator before 12 pm on day before meeting and his claim is duly admitted. Chairman may require documentary evidence of debt.
r. 2.22(1) and (3)   [No prescribed form]

2.9.6   Votes calculated according to a creditor's debt, which should be liquidated sum (although chairman can estimate a minimum entitlement).
r. 2.22 (4) and (5)

2.9.7   Chairman may admit or reject a creditor's claim for voting purposes, or mark as objected to and vote may be later declared invalid. Aggrieved creditor may appeal to court within 28 days of delivery of administrator's report on meeting.
r. 2.23

2.9.8   Secured creditor can only vote on balance of debt after deducting value of security.

There are special voting rules, on analogous principles (see rr.2.24–2.27) for:

(1)   holders of negotiable instruments

(2)   retention of title creditors

(3)   hire-purchase, conditional sale and leasing agreements.

r. 2.24

2.9.9   Resolution is passed by majority (in value) of votes in person or by proxy. A resolution is invalid if those voting against it include more than half in value of creditors to whom notice of the meeting was sent and who are not, to the best of the chairman's belief, persons connected with the company.

r. 2.28*

2.9.10   Result of meeting to be sent to all known creditors and the court and registrar of companies within 14 days. Administrator also sends progress report to creditors every 6 months, and on vacating office.

r. 2.30   [amended form 2.12]

2.9.11   There is provision for periodic revision of administrator's proposals. Essentially the same procedure is followed (statement, meeting, report) applying same rules.

s. 25

2.10   Committee of creditors

2.10.1   Creditors may resolve to form committee and elect 3–5 members who must be creditors entitled to vote at administration meetings. Committee comes into being when administrator issues certificate of due constitution. Committee meetings called by administrator at his request or request of any member (within 21 days) or as specified by committee. Administrator gives 7 days' written notice to each member (unless waived). Quorum is 2 members or representatives. Representative must have written authority. Each member has one vote; resolution on simple majority of members present. The acts of the creditors' committee are valid notwithstanding certain defects in formalities (r. 4.172A*). First meeting must be within 3 months.

s. 26

rr. 2.32–2.37*, 2.43*, 2.46 and 2.46A*   [forms 2.13, 2.14]

2.10.2   Member may resign by written notice. Membership automatically terminated if member bankrupt (replaced by his trustee) or misses 3 consecutive meetings or ceases to be a creditor. Member may be removed by resolution on 14 days' notice.

rr. 2.38–2.40

2.10.3   Administrator may, with consent, seek postal resolutions.

r. 2.43*

2.10.4   Members' reasonable travel expenses are expenses in the administration, except where meeting called at the instance of creditor within 3 months of last meeting.
r. 2.45

The liquidation committee where winding up immediately follows administration (or voluntary arrangement)

2.10.5   Where winding-up order immediately follows discharge of administration order and court appoints administrator (or supervisor) as liquidator, if there was a properly constituted creditors' committee with at least 3 members who agree to continue acting, it continues in being as liquidation committee. Committee is constituted on issue of liquidators certificate, which is filed with court. Liquidator makes first report to committee as soon as possible. Thereafter 4.44.2 – 4.44.6 below apply.
s. 140
rr. 4.173–178* (r. 4.172A*)

2.11   Company meetings

Administrator may call company meeting, the rules being similar to 2.9.3 above, otherwise as a general meeting of the company in accordance with articles and Companies Act 1985.
r. 2.31

2.12   Administrator's remuneration

2.12.1   Basis of remuneration is either:
(1)   fixed percentage of value of property or
(2)   on time costing of administrator and his staff
relevant factors:
(a)   complexity of case
(b)   any exceptional responsibility
(c)   effectiveness of administrator
(d)   value and nature of property
r. 2.47*

2.12.2   Basis of remuneration (and percentage if applicable) determined by creditors' committee (if there is one). If no committee, by creditors' meeting. In default of above, fixed by court. If administrator feels rate or amount fixed is insufficient he may apply to creditors' meeting; or to court. If administrator is a solicitor and employs his own firm, profit costs not payable to it unless authorised by committee, creditors or court.
rr. 2.47*, 2.48, 2.49*

2.12.3 Twenty-five per cent in value of creditors may apply to court to reduce administrator's remuneration if excessive. Applicant first attends *ex parte* hearing to show cause, before venue fixed. Applicant then gives 14 days notice of hearing to administrator, together with evidence in support. Costs of application paid by applicant unless court orders otherwise.

r. 2.50   [No prescribed form]

2.13   Accounting

2.13.1 Administrator must send an account of receipts and payments to the court; registrar of companies and each member of committee within 2 months of:

(1) end of each 6 month period in administration
(2) ceasing to act as administrator

r. 2.52 (1) and (2)   [form 2.15]

2.13.2 Form of account is an abstract showing:

(1) receipts and payments during relevant 6 months, or
(2) other period if appropriate

In default Administrator is liable to fine

r. 2.52 (3) and (4)   [form 2.15]

2.14   Vacation of office

2.14.1 Administrator may be removed by court order or resign. He must vacate his office if:

(1) ceases to be insolvency practitioner
(2) administration order is discharged

Remuneration and expenses payable out of company property have priority over any floating charge, as do debts and liabilities incurred while he was in office under contracts of employment. Contracts of employment are not adopted by administrators acts or omissions in first 14 days of appointment.

s. 19

2.14.2 Administrator may resign, on notice:

(1) on grounds of ill health
(2) if intention to cease practice as insolvency practitioner
(3) conflict of interest or change of personal circumstances imped-ing his duties
(4) other grounds, with leave of court.

r. 2.53   [amended forms 2.16, 2.17]

2.14.3 Administrator must give 7 days' notice to:

(1) joint administrator (if any); if not applicable, to

(2) creditors' committee; if not applicable, to
(3) company and creditors
r. 2.53(3)

2.15 Variation or discharge of order

Administrator may apply to court to discharge order or vary
specifying additional purpose if:
(1) original purposes achieved or incapable of achievement
(2) required to do so by creditors' meeting
Court may make any order it thinks fit including winding-up order
Administrator must send office copy of order to registrar of companies, and in default is liable to fines.
s. 18

2.16 Dealing with charged property

Administrator may deal with or dispose of charged property (being
subject to floating charge, hire-purchase, conditional sale, chattel
leasing agreement or retention of title). He may apply to court to
dispose of such property if it will benefit the administration. Net
proceeds of disposal (or market value) are applied to reducing the
security-holders' debt.
s. 15
r. 2.51   [No prescribed form]

2.17 Protection of interests of creditors and members

At any time when administration order is in force creditor or
member of company can apply by petition to court on the ground
(1) management by administrator is unfairly prejudicial to interests
    of all or some creditors or members (including, at least, the
    applicant), or
(2) any actual or proposed act of omission of administrator is, or
    would be, so prejudicial.
Court may make any order it thinks fit, but cannot obstruct or
overturn voluntary arrangement or compromise.
s. 27

2.18 VAT bad debt relief

Once administration order is made, creditors entitled to claim relief
if administrator issues 'Certificate of insolvency for the purposes of
Section 22 (3) (b) of the Value Added Tax Act 1983'.
rr. 2.56 – 2.58

3. Receivership

Contents*page*

3.0 Introduction

Many of the provisions of the Act relating to administrative receivers were brought into being to counter the legitimate complaints of unsecured creditors that they had no knowledge of the actions being taken by a receiver appointed by a debenture holder and no control over him. Administrative receivers do now have limited reporting obligations to unsecured creditors and these are dealt with in this chapter together with the rights of creditors to seek information.

ADMINISTRATIVE RECEIVERS

3.1 Appointment

Acceptance of appointment may be oral or in writing. If given orally within 7 days a person appointed sole or joint administrative receiver shall give written confirmation to the appointor of his acceptance. The confirmation must state:

(1) the time and date of receipt of notice of the appointment
(2) the time and date of acceptance
s. 33
r. 3.1*   [New form 3.1]

3.2   Notice and advertisement of appointment

3.2.1   Forthwith on appointment the administrative receiver sends to the
         company a notice stating the following:
         (1) the registered name and number of the company
         (2) any other name with which the company has been registered
             during the 12 months preceding that date
         (3) any trading name used by the company during those 12 months,
             if substantially different from its then registered name
         (4) the name and address of the administrative receiver and date of
             his appointment
         (5) the name of the appointor
         (6) a brief description of the debenture or other instrument and its
             date
         (7) a brief description of any assets of the company excluded from
             the appointment
         r. 3.2   [New form 3.1A]

3.2.2   Forthwith the administrative receiver must advertise a notice once in
         the Gazette and once in such newspaper as he considers most
         appropriate for ensuring it comes to the notice of the company's
         creditors. This notice must state all the matters specified in (1) – (5)
         above.
         r. 3.2(3) and (4)   [No prescribed form]

3.2.3   Within 28 days of appointment the administrative receiver must
         notify all creditors of whose addresses he is aware. This notice must
         state all matters in (1) – (7) above.
         s. 46
         r. 3.2   [No prescribed form].

3.3   Statement of affairs

3.3.1   Forthwith after appointment the administrative receiver must
         require by notice formulation of statement in the prescribed form as
         to the affairs of the company from:
         (1) present and past officers
         (2) those who have taken part at any time within the past year in the
             formation of the company
         (3) employees or those employed during the past year (or those
             employed under a contract for services)

(4) officers of any company that is, or was during the past year, itself an officer

3.3.2   The statement of affairs shall show:
(1) particulars of the company's assets, debts and liabilities
(2) the names and addresses of its creditors
(3) the securities held by creditors
(4) the dates when the securities were given
(5) the estimated deficiency/surplus as regards each class of creditor and the members
s. 47
r. 3.3(1)   [New form 3.1B]

3.3.3   The persons to whom notice is sent by the administrative receiver are called deponents.
r. 3.3(2)

3.3.4   The notice shall inform each deponent of:
(1) the names and addresses of any others to whom the notice has been sent
(2) the time within which the statement must be delivered
(3) the penalties for non-compliance (fine and daily default fine)
(4) the statutory duty of the deponent under s. 235 to provide the information
r. 3.3(3)   [New form 3.1B]

3.3.5   On request the administrative receiver must supply each deponent with the forms required for the preparation of the statement of affairs.
r. 3.3(4)*

3.3.6   The statement of affairs verified by affidavit shall be delivered by the deponent (or by one of them) to the administrative receiver. All deponents should use the same form.
r. 3.4(1)   [form 3.2]

3.3.7   The administrative receiver may require any of the persons mentioned in 3.3.1 above to submit an affidavit of concurrence, stating that he concurs in the statement of affairs. The maker of such an affidavit may qualify it where he lacks the necessary knowledge or disagrees with the statement of affairs.
r. 3.4(2) and (3)   [No prescribed form]

3.3.8   Every person making an affidavit of concurrence shall deliver it to the administrative receiver together with a copy.
r. 3.4(5)

3.3.9   The administrative receiver retains the verified statement of affairs
        and any affidavits of concurrence as part of the records of the
        receivership.
        r. 3.4(6)

3.3.10 The administrative receiver may apply to the court to limit the rights
        of inspection of the statement of affairs or any part of it if he thinks
        unlimited   inspection   would   prejudice   the   conduct   of   the
        receivership.
        r. 3.5   [No prescribed form]

3.3.11 The administrative receiver may release a deponent from the
        obligation to submit a statement of affairs or may extend a
        deponent's time for submission.
        s. 47(5)
        r. 3.6

3.3.12 If the administrative receiver refuses to grant a deponent's request
        for time or a release, the deponent may apply to the court.
        s. 47(5)
        r. 3.6(2)

3.3.13 The court may dismiss the application if it thinks the deponent has
        shown no sufficient cause but before doing so must give the
        deponent an opportunity to attend an *ex parte* hearing of which he
        has been given at least 7 days notice. If the application is not
        dismissed at this stage the court fixes a hearing date and gives notice
        to the deponent.
        r. 3.6(3)   [No prescribed form]

3.3.14 The deponent gives at least 14 days' notice of the hearing to the
        administrative receiver with a copy of the application and of any
        evidence in support.
        r. 3.6(4)   [No prescribed form]

3.3.15 The administrative receiver may file a written report of any matters
        he wishes to draw to the court's attention and gives the deponent a
        copy not later than 5 days before the hearing. The administrative
        receiver may attend on the application.
        r. 3.6(5)   [No prescribed form]

3.3.16 The deponent ususally has to pay his own costs of any application.
        r. 3.6(7)

3.3.17 The administrative receiver must pay any expenses incurred by a
        deponent making the statement of affairs and affidavit to the extent

the administrative receiver thinks reasonable, subject to appeal to the court. There appears to be no provision for payment of the expenses of an affidavit of concurrence.
r. 3.7

3.4 Report to creditors

3.4.1 Within 3 months after appointment the administrative receiver shall prepare a report on the following:
  (1) the events leading up to his appointment, so far as he is aware of them.
  (2) the disposal or proposed disposal by him of any property of the company and the carrying on or proposed carrying on of any business of the company.
  (3) the amounts of principal and interest payable to the debenture holder who appointed him and the amounts payable to preferential creditors
  (4) any amount likely to be available for payment to other creditors
  (5) summary of the statement of affairs and the administrative receiver's comments on it
The administrative receiver may exclude from the report anything which would seriously prejudice the carrying out by him of his functions.
s. 48(1), (5) and (6)

3.4.2 Within 3 months after appointment the administrative receiver sends the report to:
  (1) the registrar of companies together with a copy of the statement of affairs and any affidavits of concurrence (if these have not by then been submitted to the administrative receiver he may send them later, upon receipt)
  (2) any trustees for secured creditors
  (3) those secured creditors of whose addresses the administrative receiver is aware.
s. 48(1)

3.4.3 Within the same time and if the company is not in liquidation the administrative receiver must either:
  (1) send a copy of the report to all unsecured creditors of whose addresses he is aware, or
  (2) publish in the newspaper in which his appointment was advertised a notice giving an address to which unsecured creditors may write for a free copy of the report
and in either case, lay a copy of the report before a meeting of

unsecured creditors called on at least 14 days' notice.
s. 48(2)
r. 3.8   [form 3.3]

3.4.4   The administrative receiver may apply to the court:
         (1) to extend any of the 3 month periods referred to
         (2) to dispense with the holding of the meeting of unsecured
             creditors
         And if the administrative receiver proposes to make this application
         he shall so state in his report and the report or published notice shall
         indicate the date time and place fixed by the court for the hearing
         s. 48

3.4.5   If the company is in liquidation the administrative receiver shall
         send a copy of the report to the liquidator either:
         (1) within 7 days of sending the report to the registrar of com-
             panies, or
         (2) if the liquidator is appointed later, within 7 days of that date
         Where the administrative receiver does so within 3 months after his
         appointment he need not comply with 3.4.3 above or hold a
         creditors' meeting. The court may extend this 3 month period.
         s. 48

3.5   Creditors' meeting

3.5.1   The administrative receiver shall have regard to the convenience of
         creditors in fixing a venue for the meeting which shall take place
         between 10 am and 4 pm on a business day, unless court otherwise
         directs.
         r. 3.9(1) and (2)

3.5.2   With the notice summoning the meeting the administrative receiver
         shall send forms of proxy. The notice shall state that wholly secured
         creditors are not entitled to attend or be represented.
         r. 3.9(4) and (5) [No prescribed form of notice] proxy in form 8.3

3.5.3   Notice of the meeting shall be published in the newspaper in which
         the administrative receiver's appointment was advertised.
         r. 3.9(6)   [No prescribed form]

3.5.4   Either the administrative receiver shall be chairman of the meeting
         or a person nominated by him in writing who must be either an
         insolvency practitioner or an employee of the adminstrative receiver
         or his firm who has insolvency experience.
         r. 3.10

3.5.5   In order to vote, a creditor must, by 12 am on the business day before the meeting, give written details of the debt to the administrative receiver and lodge any proxy intended to be used.
r. 3.11

3.5.6   The chairman of the meeting may call for further evidence of a creditor's claim and may admit or reject claims for voting purposes. A partially secured creditor may vote only on the unsecured amount of his claim.
r.3.12

3.5.7   If the chairman is in doubt whether to admit or reject a claim he shall mark it as objected to and allow the creditor to vote.
r. 3.12(3)

3.5.8   The chairman's decision on admission or rejection of claims for voting is subject to appeal to the court but the creditor will usually have to bear the costs.
r. 3.12(2) and (5)

3.5.9   The meeting may not be adjourned unless the chairman thinks it desirable. If there is no quorum and the meeting is not adjourned it is deemed to have been held.
r. 3.14

3.5.10   A resolution is passed if a majority in value of those present and voting in person or by proxy have voted in favour of it.
r. 3.15(1)

3.5.11   The chairman makes a record of the meeting including a list of those creditors attending personally or by proxy and the names and addresses of those elected to be members of any creditors' committee.
r. 3.15 (2) and (3)

3.6   Creditors' committee

The creditors' meeting may resolve to establish a creditors' committee of at least 3 and not more than 5 creditors. A body corporate may be a committee member but can act only through its authorised representative.
s. 49
r. 3.16

3.6.2   The creditors' committee comes into being only when the administrative receiver has issued a certificate of due constitution.
r. 3.17(1)   [form 3.4]

3.6.3   The administrative receiver issues the certificate when at least 3 of the nominated members have agreed to act. Agreement may be given by proxy holder or representative authorised under s. 375 Companies Act 1985. As and when other members signify their agreement the administrative receiver shall issue an amended certificate.
r. 3.17(2) and (3)*   [form 3.4]

3.6.4   The certificate and any amended certificates are sent by the administrative receiver to the registrar of companies. The administrative receiver also reports any change in membership of the committee to the registrar.
r. 3.17(4) and (5)   [form 3.5]

3.6.5   The rules governing the procedure of the committee are parallel to those which apply to the creditors' committee in a liquidation (4.44.2– 4.44.6 below). Section 49(2) gives the committee power to require the administrative receiver to attend before it and give such information in relation to the receivership as it may reasonably require.
s. 49(2)
rr. 3.18 – 3.30

3.7   Resignation

3.7.1   Before resigning office the administrative receiver is required to give at least 7 days' notice of his intention to:
(1)   the person who appointed him
(2)   the company or any liquidator appointed
(3)   creditors' committee, if any
r. 3.33(1)*   [No prescribed form]

3.7.2   The notice must specify the date of intended resignation.
r. 3.33(2)

3.7.3   No notice is necessary if the administrative receiver resigns following the making of an administration order.
s. 45
r. 3.33(3)

3.8   Vacation of office

3.8.1   On completion of the receivership, or if the administrative receiver ceases to be an insolvency practitioner, the administrative receiver shall forthwith give notice of his vacating office to the company or to any liquidator and the members of the creditors' committee if any.
r. 3.35(1)*   [No prescribed form]

3.8.2   Within 14 days after vacating office the administrative receiver shall give notice to the registrar of companies.
s. 45(4)   Companies Act 1985, s. 405(2)
r. 3.35(2)   [No prescribed form]

3.8.3   If the administrative receiver dies, notice of the death must be given forthwith by the person who appointed him to:
(1)   the registrar of companies
(2)   the company or any liquidator appointed
(3)   the members (if any) of the creditors' committee
r. 3.34*   [form 3.7]

3.8.4   The administrative receiver may only be removed from office by order of the court. The person appointing him has no power to remove or replace him.
s. 45(1)

RECEIVERS

3.9   Receivers distinguished from administrative receivers

A receiver or manager appointed only over specific assets will not be affected by the provisions of the Act. He need not be an insolvency practitioner. Generally he will either be appointed under the provisions of the Law of Property Act 1925 or by the court. His powers derive either from that Act or the terms of the charge or, if appointed by the court, the terms of the order. Note that even if appointed under the Law of Property Act, if the assets covered by the appointment comprise substantially the whole of the undertaking of the company, then the receiver may be an administrative receiver and obliged to comply with the provisions of the Insolvency Act 1986.

4. Winding up

Contents

.0 Introduction

A company may be wound up voluntarily (members or creditors) or compulsorily by the court. A members' voluntary winding up is a solvent winding up but is briefly mentioned in this chapter because a significant proportion of such become creditors' voluntary winding up when it is discovered that the company is not in fact solvent.

The functions of the liquidator are to ensure that the assets of the company are got in, realised and distributed to the company's creditors and, if there is any surplus, to the persons entitled.

The Act significantly amends or clarifies the old law (pre-Insolvency Act 1985) in numerous important areas, in many cases with the intention of eradicating certain abusive practices. Some of the areas of change, which the authors consider are of regular practical application, are:

(1) time and venue of creditors' meetings
(2) voting for appointment of liquidator and resolutions
(3) appointment of liquidator by Secretary of State
(4) *Re Centrebind Ltd* [1967] 1 WLR 377
(5) conversion of members' to creditors' voluntary winding up
(6) disclaimer
(7) special manager
(8) public examination
(9) phoenix syndrome
(10) interest on debts
(11) supply of public utilities
(12) early dissolution by official receiver

WINDING UP BY THE COURT

4.1 Jurisdiction

4.1.1 High Court can wind up any company. County court has concurrent jurisdiction and similar powers where:
(1) company's paid up share capital does not exceed £120,000
(2) company's registered office in county court district of court designated as having winding up jurisdiction
However a proceeding in the wrong court is not invalid.
ss. 117, 118

4.1.2 When administration order or voluntary arrangement in being petition is presented to the court which made the administration order or to which nominees' report was submitted
r. 4.7(8)★

4.2 Application

4.2.1 Application to the court is by petition presented by: the company, directors, creditor or creditors (including contingent or prospective), contributory or contributories (in certain circumstances), or any combination thereof. The Secretary of State may present petition in certain circumstances (usually if expedient in public interest).
s. 124

4.2.2 On hearing petition court may make order, dismiss it, adjourn conditionally or unconditionally, make interim order or any other order.
s. 125

4.2.3 Grounds of Application (inter alia):
(1) special resolution of company
(2) company does not commence business within a year of incorporation or suspends business for a year

(3) company is unable to pay its debts
(4) just and equitable that company be wound up
s.122

4.2.4   Company may be wound up by the court if it is unable to pay its debts and is so deemed if:
(1) fails to comply with statutory demand, or
(2) execution is unsatisfied in whole or part, or
(3) it is proved to the satisfaction of the court that company cannot pay its debts as they fall due
(Therefore it is not strictly necessary that the debt exceed £750.)
ss. 122, 123

4.3   The statutory demand

4.3.1   Statutory demand is written demand for minimum £750 served by a creditor on the company by leaving it at the company's registered office requiring payment within 3 weeks. Must be dated and signed by creditor or person stating himself to be authorised.
s. 123
r. 4.4   [amended form 4.1]

4.3.2   Must state:
(1) amount of debt and consideration (or other way it arises)
(2) any other charge (including interest) and grounds
(3) warning of intention to wind up if payment not made
(4) time limit for payment
(5) possible methods of compliance
(6) how to contact the creditor
r. 4.5, 4.6

4.4   Petition by creditors (or company or directors)

4.4.1   File petition and verifying affidavit in court. Fee currently £40 + £240 deposit toward official receiver's costs (repayable if funds available; not repayable if petition struck out). Court fixes hearing and seals petition and copy petition(s) as appropriate (see 4.4.6 below).
r. 4.7*   [forms 4.2, 4.3]

4.4.2   Serve sealed copy petition on company (not necessary if company is petitioner). Personal service at registered office or intended registered office or, if no registered office, at last known principal place of business:
(1) by handing to director, officer or employee of company or authorised person present, or
(2) depositing it where it will come to notice
If service at registered office is not practicable, or no registered

office, or unregistered company, serve at last known place of business in such manner that it is likely to come to notice; or deliver to secretary, a director, manager or other principal officer (wherever such person may be found).

(3) if overseas company, per s. 695 of the Companies Act 1985
(4) if above methods fail, apply to court *ex parte* on affidavit for substituted service order

r. 4.8*

4.4.3   File affidavit of service exhibiting sealed copy petition (and sealed copy of order of substituted service if applicable) immediately after service.

r. 4.9   [form 4.4 or 4.5]

4.4.4   Advertise once in the Gazette not less than 7 business days after service nor less than 7 business days before hearing. Send copy petition to recognised advertising agent who will comply with rules as to form of advertisement. Court may dismiss petition not properly advertised.

r. 4.11   [form 4.6]

4.4.5   Verifying affidavit is prima facie evidence of statements in petition. Exhibit petition. Deponent to be petitioner or officer or solicitor of petitioner or authorised person, having knowledge of matters in petition. If deponent is not petitioner, state his capacity, authority and means of knowledge.

r. 4.12   [form 4.3]

4.4.6   Send copies of petition immediately after service on company, as appropriate to:

(1) administrator
(2) administrative receiver
(3) liquidator (if company in voluntary liquidation)
(4) supervisor of any voluntary arrangement
(5) Bank of England if company is a bank or is or was an authorised institution within the meaning of the Banking Act 1987

r. 4.10*

4.4.7   Other persons entitled to copy of petition upon request with copying fee are: any director, contributory or creditor.

r. 4.13

4.4.8   Certificate of compliance to be filed by petitioner or solicitor at least 5 days before hearing. Certificate will show:

(1) date of presentation of petition

(2) date fixed for hearing
(3) date of service
(4) that advertisement complied with rules (file copy of advertisement with certificate)
Court may dismiss if this rule not complied with.
r. 4.14   [form 4.7]

5   Withdrawal of petition

Petitioner applies *ex parte* for hearing at least 5 days before hearing of petition; must satisfy the court:
(1) petition not been advertised
(2) has received no notices (in support or opposition)
(3) company consents to withdrawal
Court may make order giving leave to withdraw (costs to be agreed).
r. 4.15   [form 4.8]

6   Notice of list of appearances

.6.1   Person (usually creditor) intending to appear at hearing of petition shall give notice to petitioner specifying:
(1) his name, address, telephone number and reference (or solicitor or agent)
(2) amount and nature of debt
Notice to arrive before 4 pm day before hearing (or adjourned hearing). In default such person may appear only with leave of court.
r. 4.16   [form 4.9]

.6.2   Petitioner prepares list of supporting or opposing creditors who have given notice with details and hands it into court before hearing of petition. If no such persons, state none.
r. 4.17   [form 4.10]

.6.3   If company opposes petition, it files affidavit in opposition not less than 7 days before hearing, and sends copy to petitioner.
r. 4.18

7   Substitution of creditor or contributory

Where a petition is discontinued at the hearing, but has not been withdrawn as in 4.5 above, a creditor or contributory wishing to prosecute the petition may be substituted on such terms as court thinks just (usually reserve, re-verify and, if appropriate re-advertise). Usually occurs where petitioner had been paid off before hearing or debt is properly disputed. Creditor or contributory may apply whether or not petitioner appears at hearing.
r. 4.19

4.8 The winding-up order

4.8.1 Upon making of winding-up order the court informs the offici receiver who becomes liquidator, unless previous administrator c supervisor of voluntary arrangement is appointed. Court sends copies of sealed order to official receiver who serves copy o company and sends copy to registrar of companies. Official receive forthwith advertises in the Gazette and one local newspaper.
s. 130
rr. 4.20, 4.21*   [form 4.11; amended forms 4.12, 4.13]

4.8.2 No action or proceedings against the company or its property ma commence or continue except with leave of court.
s. 130(2)

4.8.3 Winding up is deemed to commence at time of presentation c petition, unless earlier resolution passed by company.
s. 129

4.9 Petition to wind up by contributories

4.9.1 Petition specifying grounds and nature of relief sought filed wit court with one service copy and deposit.
r. 4.22(1)*   [amended form 4.14]

4.9.2 Court fixes date for directions hearing in chambers endorsed o sealed petition. Petitioner serves on company at least 14 days befor hearing.
r. 4.22(2) – (4)

4.9.3 Court gives directions as to service, procedure, advertisement evidence and any other matters.
r. 4.23

4.9.4 The rules in 4.6.1 and 4.6.2 above apply, with necessary modif cation.
rr. 4.21A, 4.24

4.9A Petition by administrator or supervisor

4.9A.1 Petition filed at instance of company's administrator shall
(1) be expressed to be petition of company by its administrator
(2) name administrator, number of administration petition an date of order

(3)   contain application under s. 18 requesting administration order be discharged and court make any consequential order it thinks fit.

4.9A.2   Petition presented by supervisor of voluntary arrangement or at instance of administrator is treated as if petition by contributories and Rules apply accordingly.

4.9A.3   Jurisdiction: see 4.1.2.

4.9A.4   Where petition seeks appointment of former supervisor or administrator as liquidator, that person files report with court 2 days before petiiton return date including particulars of
(1)   date he notified creditors of such intention (10 days earlier)
(2)   details of creditors' response including any objections to his appointment.

4.9A.5   If winding up order made pursuant to petition presented when voluntary arrangement was in force, the proper expenses of the administration of the voluntary arrangement are a first charge on the company's assets.
s. 140
rr. 4.7*, 4.21A

4.10   Appointment of provisional liquidator

4.10.1   Provisional liquidator may be appointed by court between presentation of petition and making of winding-up order. Official receiver or other fit person may be provisional liquidator.
s. 135

4.10.2   Application may be by petitioner, creditor, contributory or company, or any person who would be entitled to petition.
r. 4.25(1)

4.10.3   Affidavit in support will state:
(1)   grounds for application
(2)   proposed provisional liquidator, if not official receiver, name, qualification (insolvency practitioner) and consent of person to act
(3)   whether or not official receiver has been informed of application
(4)   whether, to applicant's knowledge, there is any voluntary liquidator, administrative receiver or voluntary arrangement
(5)   estimate of value of assets
r. 4.25(2)   [No prescribed form]

4.10.4   Applicant sends copies of application and affidavit to official reciever
         who may appear at hearing (official receiver must have opportunity
         of appearing).
         r. 4.25(3)*

4.10.5   Where provisional liquidator is appointed court gives notice to
         official receiver and to provisional liquidator if different.
         r. 4.25A   [new form: 4.14A]

4.10.6   Order appointing provisional liquidator will specify his functions
         and may limit his powers. Court sends sealed copies of order to
         official receiver, person appointed and administrative receiver as
         appropriate. Provisional liquidator then sends copies to company
         and voluntary liquidator if any.
         s. 135
         r. 4.26   [form 4.15]

4.10.7   If official receiver is appointed, applicant must deposit with him or
         provide security for his costs, as court directs. If this proves
         insufficient, official receiver may apply for increase. Deposit is
         repaid if winding-up order is subsequently made and company has
         sufficient assets.
            If insolvency practitioner is appointed he provides security (at first
         instance) but:
         (1) if winding-up order not made, he is reimbursed by company
         (2) if winding-up order is made, he is reimbursed out of assets
         r. 4.27, 4.28

4.10.8   Remuneration of provisional liquidator is fixed by court, on his
         application, having regard to similar criteria to criteria in 4.20
         below. If a winding up order is not made the provisional liquidator's
         remuneration and expenses are reimbursed out of the property of
         the company.
         r. 4.30*

4.10.9   Appointment of provisional liquidator is terminated:
         (1) on dismissal of petition, or
         (2) any person mentioned in 4.10.2 above may apply to court and
              court makes any directions it thinks fit.
         r. 4.31*

4.11   Statement of affairs

4.11.1   When winding-up order made or provisional liquidator appointed,
         official receiver will require formulation of statement of affairs by
         some or all of:

    (1) present or past officers of company (including voluntary liquidator)

    (2) anyone involved in the company's formation if within one year previous to order

    (3) present or past employees (within one year previous)

    (4) present or past officers or employees of another company which is or was within one year an officer of the company.

(Such persons are referred to as deponents.)

s. 131(3)

4.11.2 Statement will include particulars of company's assets, debts and liabilities, names and addresses of creditors, securities held by creditors and the dates when securities were given; and any other information official receiver requires. Must be in proper form.

s. 131 (2)   [form 4.17]

4.11.3 Official receiver sends notice to deponents he considers appropriate requiring them to submit statement within 21 days. The notice must inform each deponent of:

    (1) details of other deponents to whom notice sent

    (2) time limit for delivery of statement

    (3) deponent's legal duty to provide information or attend official receiver required and penalty for non-compliance (fines).

s. 131 (7)

r. 4.32   [amended form 4.16]

4.11.4 Deponent must verify statement of affairs by affidavit (included in form 4.17) (may be sworn before official receiver) and official receiver may require any other potential deponent to submit affidavit of concurrence (which may be qualified). Official receiver then files verified statement (and any affidavit of concurrence) with court.

r 4.33

4.11.5 If official receiver thanks that disclosure of whole or part of statement of affairs may prejudice liquidation he may apply to court for order to limit disclosure.

r. 4.35

4.11.6 Official receiver may release deponent from obligation (or extend time) or deponent may apply to court, usually at his own cost.

r. 4.36

4.11.7 If any deponent cannot himself prepare a proper statement of affairs (or affidavit of concurrence) official receiver may make allowance out of assets to provide assistance by solicitor or accountant approved by official receiver.

r. 4.37

4.12   Submission of accounts

4.12.1   Official receiver may require up to 3 years' accounts or to last audit if earlier (verified on affidavit if necessary) from any person specified in s.235 (3), being those mentioned in 4.11.1 above but specifically including those employed under a contract for services and any administrator, administrative receiver or voluntary liquidator as appropriate (see also 5.3 below.) Official receiver may apply to court for accounts of earlier period. Expenses are covered as in 4.11.7 above. Official receiver files copy with court.
r. 4.39

4.12.2   Official receiver can at any time require, within 21 days, further information or explanation of matters referred to in statement of affairs or accounts, to be verified on affidavit if official receiver so requests.
r.4.42

4.13   Report by official receiver

4.13.1   Official receiver sends to creditors and contributories report of winding-up proceedings and state of company's affairs, including summary of any statement of affairs, unless statement of affairs does not materially alter position previously reported. Official receiver must report at least once to creditors, and file copy report(s) with court.
rr. 4.43*, 4.45, 4.46

4.13.2   If official receiver decides not to call meetings, he gives notice of his decision to creditors, contributories and court.
r.45(2)

4.13.3   Official receiver may apply to court to relieve him of duty to report or to carry out duty other than specified in 4.13.1 above having regard to costs, company assets and interest of creditors or contributories. If winding up stayed by court order, official receiver need not report.
rr. 4.47, 4.48

4.13.4   It is duty of official receiver to investigate:
(1) generally the promotion, formation, business, dealings and affairs of company
(2) causes of failure
and to make report (if any) to the court as he thinks fit. See 12.5.6 below.
s. 132(1)

4.14   Meetings of creditors and contributories

First meetings

4.14.1   Official receiver may elect to remain as liquidator or call meetings of creditors and contributories within 12 weeks of order to nominate another liquidator. Official receiver gives 21 days' notice of appropriate meeting to creditors and contributories. Notice to creditors will specify when proofs and proxies (for voting purposes) must be lodged by; and to contributors when proxies must be lodged by; in each case not more than 4 days before meeting. (Proxies: see chapter 10.) Notice of meetings also advertised. Creditors of 25 per cent in value can request official receiver to call first meetings (then notice in 4.13.2 above is withdrawn).
s. 136
r. 4.50   [form 4.21]

4.14.2   Business of first meetings is limited to resolutions:
(1)   to appoint liquidator (or joint liquidators)
(2)   to establish liquidation committee
(3)   to specify liquidator's remuneration (or defer consideration)
(4)   to specify position of joint liquidators inter se
(5)   in case of a requisitioned meeting, to authorise payment of costs of meetings out of assets
(6)   to adjourn for maximum 3 weeks
(7)   any other resolution if special reasons
r. 4.52

Liquidator's power to call meetings

4.14.3   Official receiver or liquidator may call subsequent meetings of creditors and/or contributories for purposes of ascertaining their wishes. Twenty-one days' notice of meeting specifying time for lodging proofs and proxies, not more than 4 days before meeting.
r. 4.54   [forms 4.22, 4.23]

4.14.4   Chairman of meeting is:
(1)   Official receiver or another official receiver or deputy official receiver nominated in writing, or
(2)   liquidator or person nominated in writing being an insolvency practitioner or employee of liquidator experienced in insolvency matters.
r. 4.55

Requisitioned meetings

4.14.5   Creditors of 25 per cent in value can request liquidator to call
meeting of creditors or contributories. Contributories may requisition contributories' meeting. Request accompanied by:
(1) list of concurring creditors (if applicable) showing value
(2) written confirmation of their concurrence
(3) statement of purpose of proposed meeting
   Person seeking meeting must deposit with liquidator security for
expense of meeting but meeting of creditors may resolve that
expenses be in liquidation.
   Liquidator fixes meeting within 35 days of request, giving 21 days'
notice.
s. 136(5)
r. 4.57   [forms 4.21, 4.24]

4.14.6   Attendance of company's personnel (present and past officers,
employees etc) can be required by liquidator. One or more of
company's personnel (and other persons) may attend meetings,
having given notice, at discretion of chairman. Questions may be put
to company's personnel at chairman's discretion.
r. 4.58

4.14.7   Meetings to be held between 10 am and 4 pm on business day at
venue convenient to persons invited. Proxy form sent with notice.
r. 4.60   [form 8.4 or 8.5]

Resolutions

4.14.8   Resolution is passed by majority (in value) of votes in person or by
proxy. Resolution for appointment of liquidator: 4.18.1 below
applies (overall majority).
r. 4.63*

4.14.9   Chairman may suspend meetings for one hour. Chairman may
adjourn meeting at his discretion, or resolution may adjourn meeting
(subject to 9.3 below). If no quorum within 30 minutes of commencement of meeting, chairman may, at his discretion, adjourn
meeting to such time and place as he may appoint. Maximum
adjournment 21 days in each case.
r. 4.65*

Quorum

4.14.10 Now see 10.6 below.
rr. 4.66, 12.4A

Entitlement to vote

4.14.11 Creditor may only vote if:
(1) he has lodged proof of debt as required by notice and proof admitted
(2) proxy lodged as required by notice
Votes calculated according to a creditor's debt, which should be liquidated sum (although chairman can estimate minimum entitlement).

Secured creditor can only vote on balance of debt after deducting value of security as estimated by him. At contributories meeting voting rights are as at general meeting (subject to articles). As to form of voting to elect liquidator, see 4.18.1 below. Contributories' voting rights are as at general meeting.
rr. 4.67 – 4.4.69

Admission and rejection of proof at creditors' meeting

4.14.12 Chairman may admit or reject a creditor's claim for voting purposes, or mark it as objected to and vote may be later declared invalid. Aggrieved creditor may appeal to court, but chairman is not liable in costs unless court so orders.
r. 4.70

4.14.13 Chairman makes and keeps minutes of meeting, attendance list and record of resolutions, and files particulars of resolution with court.
r. 4.71

The liquidation committee

4.14.14 Liquidation committee may be appointed at first meetings or at subsequent meetings which liquidator may call or 10 per cent of creditors may requisition for purpose of appointing committee.
s. 141(2)

4.14.15 If creditors' meeting does not appoint committee, contributories may apply to court for order that liquidator summon a further creditors' meeting, and if such creditors' meeting shall not appoint committee, contributories may appoint committee of 3–5 of their number.
s. 141(3)

4.14.16 No liquidation committee when official receiver liquidator but committee's functions are vested in Secretary of State.
s. 141(5)

4.14.17 See 2.10.5 above on liquidation committee where winding up immediately follows administration or voluntary arrangement. And see generally 4.44 below.

4.15   Procedure for proving debts

4.15.1 Creditor wishing to recover his debt must submit written proof of debt in proper form to liquidator (subject to 4.14.12 above). (Crown may use other form.) Creditor bears cost of proving his debt.
r. 4.73, 4.78   [form 4.25]

4.15.2 Liquidator sends forms of proof to all known creditors with his first notice to creditors.
r. 4.74

4.15.3 Proof of debt will state:
(1) creditor's name and address
(2) amount of claim at date of liquidation
(3) whether interest included
(4) whether VAT included
(5) whether any part is preferential
(6) details of any security
(7) how and when debt incurred
(8) name, address and authority of signatory
(9) which documents (if any) substantiate debt
Liquidator may call to see documentary or other evidence of debt; or require verification on affidavit of debt.
rr. 4.75, 4.77   [forms, 4.25, 4.26]

4.15.4 Liquidator will allow inspection of proofs by:
(1) creditor who has submitted proof (and not rejected) or his agent
(2) contributory, or his agent
r. 4.79

4.15.5 Proof may be admitted for dividend as to whole or part. If liquidator rejects proof in whole or part, he sends statement of reasons to creditor who may apply to court within 21 days if dissatisfied with decision. Applicant sends notice of hearing to liquidator who files proof and his statement of rejection.
rr. 4.82, 4.83   [No prescribed form]

4.15.6 Creditor may at any time withdraw or vary proof with agreement of liquidator.
r. 4.84

4.15.7 Liquidator (or another creditor) may apply to court if he thinks a proof has been wrongly admitted or ought be reduced.
r. 4.85

4.16 Quantification of claims

4.16.1 Liquidator estimates value of any unliquidated debt and may revise estimate in light of further information, informing creditor accordingly.
r. 4.86

4.16.2 Creditor holding negotiable instrument must produce it, or certified copy, upon request.
r. 4.87

4.16.3 Liquidator deducts any proper discount that company entitled to.
r. 4.89

4.16.4 Mutual credits or debts are set off as appropriate, and balance (if any) is provable.
r. 4.90

4.16.5 Foreign currency debts are converted into sterling at official exchange rate at date of order.
r. 4.91

4.16.6 Rent or other periodical payments are calculated to date of order.
r. 4.92

4.16.7 Interest-bearing debts are calculated to date of order. (Interest not previously reserved or agreed may be payable in certain circumstances.) For all the purposes of the Act and the Rules the maximum rate of interest chargeable is the rate specified in s. 17 of the Judgment Act 1838 on the date company went into liquidation. See also 4.52 below.
r. 4.93*

4.16.8 Future debts may be proved subject to adjustment if dividend paid before due date.
r. 4.94

4.17 Proof by secured creditors

4.17.1 Secured creditor estimates value of his security at date of order and may revise his estimate with agreement of liquidator or leave of

court. But if he is petitioner and has valued security in petition or has voted on unsecured balance, can only re-value with leave of court.
r. 4.95

4.17.2   If secured creditor does not disclose his security in his proof, security is surrendered (may apply to court for relief if honest mistake).
r. 4.96

4.17.3   Liquidator may redeem security on 28 days' notice to secured creditor who may within 21 days seek to re-value (as mentioned in 4.17.1 above).
r. 4.97

4.17.4   If liquidator does not accept secured creditor's estimate of value he may test security by offering property for sale.
r.4.98

4.17.5   If secured creditor who has valued his security subsequently realises it, the net amount realised is substituted for his previous valuation. May prove for balance of his debt.
rr. 4.88, 4.99

4.18   Appointment of liquidator

4.18.1   Meetings of creditors and contributories nominate person to be liquidator, the creditors' nomination being preferred. If different persons nominated, any contributory or creditor may within 7 days apply to court for joint liquidation or appointment of some other person.

   If at a meeting, more than one person is nominated to be liquidator, there will be a vote. If candidate receives clear majority in value of votes available at meeting (in person or proxy) he is appointed. If no candidate receives overall majority, a further vote is taken excluding any candidate who has withdrawn or, if none has withdrawn, the candidate receiving least support on previous vote.
s. 139
rr. 4.63(2)*, 4.63(2A)

4.18.2   Where winding-up order immediately follows administration or voluntary arrangement court may appoint administrator or supervisor as liquidator.
s. 140

18.3 Where liquidator is appointed by committee of creditors (or contributories):
   (1) chairman certifies appointment (upon receiving written statement of qualified insolvency practitioner who consents to act) and the certificate is proof of appointment and authority
   (2) certificate sent to official receiver who files it with court – effective date of appointment – endorsed copy sent to liquidator, which is proof of appointment and authority
   r. 4.100   [forms 4.27, 4.28]

18.4 Where court appoints liquidator:
   (1) order not issued until liquidator files statement
   (2) appointment effective from date of order
   (3) sealed order is proof of appointment
   (4) liquidator sends notice of order to all known creditors and contributories within 28 days (or advertises if court so directs)
   (5) notice or advertisement states whether he intends to call meeting(s) to elect committee(s), or informs creditors of their power to requisition such a meeting
   r. 4.102   [forms 4.29, 4.30]

18.5 Within 14 days of appointment liquidator advertises his appointment in the Gazette and one newspaper most appropriate for ensuring it comes to notice of creditors and contributories (reimbursed from assets) and notifies registrar of companies. Liable to fine in default.
   s. 109
   r. 4.106   [form 4.31]

18.6 Where official receiver is liquidator he may at any time apply to Secretary of State for appointment of external liquidator in his place. Liquidator notifies creditors of his appointment stating whether he proposes to call creditors' meeting to appoint liquidation committee, or if not, informing creditors that they may requisition such a meeting.
   s. 137
   r. 4.104

19   Vacation of office by liquidator

Resignation

19.1 Liquidator calls creditors' meeting for purpose of his resignation, giving notice to creditors and official receiver, together with summary of receipts and payments and statement of reconciliation with

account held by Secretary of State. If no quorum present at
meeting, meeting is deemed to have been held and resolution
deemed to have been passed (but resolution replaced by written
statement).
r. 4.108*   [form 4.22]

4.19.2   Grounds for resignation are:
         (1)   ill health
         (2)   intends to cease practice as insolvency practitioner
         (3)   conflict of interest or change of personal circumstances imped
               ing his duties
         (4)   in the case of one joint liquidator, that joint liquidation no
               longer expedient.
         r. 4.108 (4) and (5)

4.19.3   If creditors' meeting resolves:
         (1)   to accept liquidator's resignation, or
         (2)   that new liquidator be appointed, or
         (3)   that resigning liquidator not be given release
         chairman sends copy of resolution to official receiver within 3 days
         together with certificate of appointment of new liquidator if appro
         priate.
         r. 4.109 (2)

4.19.4   If resignation is accepted, liquidator sends notice with account to
         official receiver who files copy with court: effective date of resig
         nation. New liquidator advertises his appointment as such.
         r.4.109 (4)   [form 4.32]

4.19.5   If creditors' meeting does not accept resignation, liquidator may
         apply to court for leave to resign. Liquidator sends copy of order to
         registrar of companies and notice to official receiver.
         r. 4.111   [forms 4.34, 4.36]

Removal of liquidator by creditors

4.19.6   Where a creditor requisitions a creditors' meeting to remove liquida
         tor, notice will state purpose(s) of meeting. Copy notice sent to
         official receiver. Creditor may apply to court to regulate summoning
         and conduct of meeting. Meeting may elect chairman other than
         liquidator, but if liquidator is chairman and resolution proposed for
         his removal, he may not adjourn meeting without consent of at least
         50 per cent in value of creditors present (in person or by proxy), and
         entitled to vote.
         s. 174(4)
         r. 113 (1)–(3)   [form 4.22]

4.19.7   Chairman sends certificate of removal to official receiver. (See 4.18
          above if new liquidator appointed.) Resolution is effective from date
          official receiver files certificate in court. Official receiver will not file
          certificate until he receives certification that removed liquidator has
          reconciled his account with that held by Secretary of State.
          rr. 4.113, 4.116   [form 4.37]

          Removal of liquidator by the court

4.19.8   Where an application is made to the court:
          (1)   for removal of liquidator, or
          (2)   order directing liquidator to summon creditors' meeting (to
                remove him)
          applicant first attends *ex parte* hearing to show cause before venue is
          fixed. Court may require applicant to provide security for liquida-
          tor's costs, and costs not usually payable out of assets. Order
          removing liquidator may include such provision as court thinks fit
          with regard to circumstances of removal.
          s. 172
          r.4.119   [form 4.39]

4.19.9   The Secretary of State may direct the removal of the liquidator.
          s. 172(4)
          r. 4.123

          Release of resigning or removed liquidator

4.19.10   From time it is effective, release discharges liquidator from all
          liability for his acts and omissions (but subject to s.212 malpractice
          provisions).
          s. 174(6)

4.19.11   Where liquidator resigns or is removed by creditors' meeting and
          release not resolved against, it is effective when relevant certificate
          filed in court.
          s. 174(4)

4.19.12   Where creditors' meeting resolves against release (on resignation or
          removal) or upon removal by court, liquidator must apply to
          Secretary of State for his release. Release effective when certificate
          filed in court.
          r. 4.121   [form 4.41]

Release on completion of administration

4.19.13 Where official receiver is still acting liquidator at completion of liquidation, he sends notice to all creditors who proved, together with summary of his receipts and payments. Official receiver applies to Secretary of State for his release.
r. 4.124

4.19.14 Liquidator (other than official receiver) calls final meeting of creditors on 28 days notice to all creditors who have proved; and notice gazetted.
Liquidator's report to meeting includes:
(1) summary of receipts and payments
(2) statement that he has reconciled account with Secretary of State.
Creditors may question liquidator and resolve against his release. Liquidator then reports by notice to court with copy to official receiver.
Release is effective when notice filed unless resolution against release, then liquidator applies to Secretary of State for release.
r. 4.125   [forms 4.22, 4.42]

4.19.15 Upon vacating office liquidator must immediately deliver up to new liquidator:
(1) the assets (less proper expenses and distributions made)
(2) records of liquidator
(3) company's books and records
Where liquidator vacates office after final meeting of creditors he delivers up any remaining papers and records to official receiver.
s. 172(8)
r. 4.138*

4.19.16 Liquidator must vacate office if he ceases to be insolvency practitioner.
s. 172(5)

4.19.17 Where liquidator intends to vacate office he must give notice (together with notice of any creditors' meeting) to official receiver, including details of any property remaining in the liquidation.
r. 4.137*

4.20 Liquidator's remuneration

4.20.1 Basis of remuneration is either:
(1) fixed percentage of value of assets realised or distributed, or

(2) on time-costing of liquidator and his staff
relevant factors:
(a) complexity of case
(b) any exceptional responsibility
(c) effectiveness of liquidator
(d) value and nature of assets
r. 4.127

4.20.2 Where liquidator is other than official receiver, basis of remuneration (and percentage, if applicable) is determined by liquidation committee, if there is one; If none by creditors' meeting; If none, in accordance with official receiver's scale.
r. 4.127(3) and (5)

4.20.3 Joint liquidators agree apportionment inter se. If dispute between them refer to the court or liquidation committee or creditors' committee.
r. 4.128

4.20.4 If liquidator considers his remuneration fixed by liquidation committee is inadequate, he may apply to creditor's meeting for increase. If liquidator considers his remuneration determined by any means in 4.20.2 above is inadequate, he may apply to the court for increase.
rr. 4.129, 4.130

4.20.5 Twenty-five per cent in value of creditors may apply to court to reduce liquidators' remuneration if considered excessive. Applicant first attends *ex parte* hearing to show cause, before venue fixed. Applicant then gives 14 days notice of hearing to liquidator, together with evidence in support. Costs of application paid by applicant unless court orders otherwise.
r. 4.131

4.21 List of contributories and calls

4.21.1 As soon as may be after appointment, liquidator exercises courts' power to settle list of contributories identifying classes of shares and contributories with details. Liquidator then gives notice of list to contributories. If contributory objects to any entry or omission, inform liquidator within 21 days. If liquidator declines to amend list, contributory may apply to court within 21 days of liquidators' reply.
s. 148
rr. 4.196, 4.199

4.21.2 Liquidator obtains sanction of liquidation committee (on *ex parte* application) to make calls. Payment of amount due may be enforced by court order.

rr. 4.203, 4.205   [forms 4.56 – 4.59]

4.21.3   If at any time before or after winding-up order it appears that a contributory is about to quit the United Kingdom remove or conceal his assets to avoid call, court may order arrest of contributory and seizure of certain assets.

s. 158

4.22   Public examination of company officers and others

4.22.1   At any time before dissolution official receiver may apply to court for public examination of any of the following persons:
(1) present or past officer of the company
(2) person who acted as liquidator, administrator, receiver or manager
(3) any other person involved in promotion formation or management of company

s. 133 (1)

4.22.2   Fifty per cent in value of creditors or 75 per cent in value of contributories can request official receiver to make application.

s. 133 (2)

4.22.3   Persons who may take part in public examination and put questions are:
(1) official receiver
(2) liquidator
(3) special manager
(4) any creditor who has proved
(5) any contributory

It is no longer a pre-condition that official receiver must first make report alleging fraud. Failure to atttend public examination without reasonable excuse is contempt of court.

ss. 133 (4), 134 (1)

4.22.4   Details of the procedure are contained in rr. 4.211 – 4.217 with appropriate forms (forms 4.61, 4.64, 4.66 and 4.67 are now amended). It remains to be seen whether the procedure will be frequently used by official receiver.

4.23 Grounds for voluntary winding up

4.23.1 Voluntary winding up is possible in the following circumstances
(1) if event occurs which articles provide is cause to dissolve and resolution to wind up voluntarily is passed at general meeting
(2) upon special resolution to wind up voluntarily
(3) upon extraordinary resolution to wind up voluntarily by reason of company's liabilities
s. 84(1)

4.23.2 Notice of resolution:
(1) copy of resolution to be sent to registrar of companies within 15 days
(2) advertise in the Gazette within 14 days
In default, responsible officer(s) liable to fine.
s. 85

4.24 Commencement of winding up

4.24.1 Voluntary winding up deemed to commence when appropriate resolution passed. Consequences:
(1) must cease business except as necessary for benefit of winding up
(2) but corporate state and powers continue until dissolution
(3) transfer of shares without liquidator's consent is void
(4) alteration in status of members is void
ss. 86 – 88

4.24.2 If company meeting to resolve to wind up is adjourned, any resolution passed at subsequent s. 98 creditors' meeting held before adjourned company meeting only takes effect upon passing of resolution by company.
r. 4.53A

4.25 Declaration of solvency

4.25.1 Directors (or majority of them) make statutory declaration that they have made a full enquiry into the company's affairs and, having done so, they have formed the opinion that the company will be able to pay its debts in full together with interest at the official rate within a period not exceeding 12 months from commencement of winding up s. 89(1)

4.25.2 Declaration must:
  (1) be made *not* more than 5 weeks before resolution passed at general meeting
  (2) include latest practicable statement of assets and liabilities
  (3) be sent to registrar of companies within 15 days of resolution
  s. 89(2) and (3)   [amended form 4.70]

4.25.3 Director making such declaration without reasonable grounds for opinion of solvency liable to imprisonment and/or fine. Presumption of no reasonable grounds if company fails to pay debts (with interest) within specified period.
  s.89 (4) and (5)

4.26 Appointment of liquidator and vacancy

4.26.1 General meeting by ordinary resolution appoints liquidator, who is insolvency practitioner who consents to act, whereupon directors' powers cease unless general meeting or liquidator sanction their continuance. Liquidator provides written statement that he is qualified insolvency practitioner. Chairman certificates appointment: proof of authority. Liquidator sends notice to creditors within 28 days.
  s. 91
  rr. 4.139, 4.141   [Forms 4.27, 4.28]

4.26.2 If vacancy occurs by death, resignation or otherwise, general meeting may appoint new liquidator (subject to any arrangement with its creditors). General meeting may be convened by any contributory or continuing joint liquidator (if any).
  s. 92

4.27 Application of the Rules

4 27.1 The following rules apply as in creditors voluntary winding up:
  (1) proof of debts: see 4.15 above
  (2) quantification: see 4.16 above
  (3) secured creditors: see 4.17 above
  (4) disclaimer: see 4.46 below
  (5) special manager: see 4.47 below
  (6) liquidators statement to registrar of companies: see 4.38.12 below
  r. 4.1*

4.27.2 The following provisions (inter alia) apply as in any winding up:
   (1) court's power to set aside certain transactions: see 4.43 below
   (2) rule against solicitation: see 4.43 below
   (3) court's general power to remove and appoint liquidator: see 4.53 below
   (4) time limits: see 4.55 below
   s. 108
   r. 4.1*

4.27.3 There are special rules as to the liquidator (rr. 4.139–148) and his remuneration (r. 4.148A*); and distribution (r. 4.182A*).

4.28 Meetings

4.28.1 If winding up continues for more than 12 months, liquidator must call general meeting of company within 3 months (and of each succeeding year end) to report on liquidation.
   s. 93

4.28.2 Liquidator calls final meeting prior to dissolution to report on conduct of liquidation and distribution of property. Advertise in the Gazette one month before meeting. Report with return to registrar of companies within 7 days of meeting. Company automatically dissolved 3 months thereafter; no application to court.
   ss. 94, 201

4.29 Conversion of creditors' voluntary winding-up

4.29.1 If liquidator forms opinion that company is insolvent, i.e. will be unable to pay its debts in full, with interest, within period stated in declaration of solvency, he must:
   (1) within 28 days call creditors' meeting to be held (in accordance with 4.30.4 and 4.30.5 below) sending each creditor at least 7 days notice.
   (2) advertise once in the Gazette
   (3) advertise in newspaper, local to company's principal place of business
   (4) provide (free) such information to creditors as they reasonably require
   (5) prepare statement of affairs for creditors' meeting (see 4.31 below
   (6) attend and preside at creditors' meeting
   (7) send copy of statement of affairs to registrar of companies within 7 days of meeting
   s. 95

4.29.2   Applicable are 4.30.4, 4.30.5 (with necessary modifications) 4.30.9
         and 4.30.10 below.

4.29.3   From the day on which the creditors' meeting is held under s.95 the
         winding up becomes a creditors' voluntary winding up.
         s. 96

CREDITORS VOLUNTARY WINDING UP

4.30   Meeting of creditors

4.30.1   Company must call creditors meeting to be held not more than 14
         days after company general meeting when resolution for voluntary
         winding up is proposed, sending at least 7 days' notice to each
         creditor (but see also 4.30.18 below).
         s. 98 (1)   [form 4.22]

4.30.2   Advertise notice once in the Gazette and in two newspapers local to
         company's principal place of business.
         s. 98 (1) (c)

4.30.3   Notice must state either:
         (1) name and address of (proposed liquidator) who will provide
             (free) such information to creditors as they reasonably require
             or
         (2) place in relevant locality where list of creditors may be
             inspected during the 2 business days before meeting
         s. 98 (2)

4.30.4   Notice must also specify venue and time (not earlier than 12 am on
         business day before meeting) by which creditors must lodge proof
         and proxies necessary to entitle them to vote at the meeting.
         r. 4.51*

4.30.5   Business at creditors' meeting is as set out in 4.14.2 except (5).
         Director is chairman at meeting. Statement of affairs laid before
         meeting. Reasonable and necessary expense of meeting is payable
         from assets; and meeting or, if payment later, liquidation commit-
         tee, must be informed of details.
         s. 99(1)
         rr. 4.53, 4.62

4.30.6   Liquidator's general power to call meetings is as 4.14.3 above.

4.30.7   Chairman at meetings of creditors or contributories is liquidator or
         person nominated in writing being an insolvency practitioner or

employee of liquidator experienced in insolvency matters (except as 4.30.5 above where director is chairman).
r. 4.56

4.30.8 Requisitioned meetings are as 4.14.5 above (25 per cent in value of creditors can requisition).

4.30.9 Attendance of company's personnel at meetings is as 4.14.6 above.

4.30.10 Venue is as 4.14.7 above (convenient time and place).

4.30.11 Resolution is generally as in 4.14.8 above (majority in value). But resolution for appointment of liquidator is as in 4.18.1 above (overall majority).

4.30.12 Suspension and adjournment is as in 4.14.9 above.

4.30.13 Quorum is as in 4.14.10 above.

4.30.14 Entitlement to vote is as in 4.14.11 above, but chairman may allow creditor to vote notwithstanding that he has failed to submit proof of debt in time, if beyond creditor's control.
r. 4.68

4.30.15 Admission and rejections of proof at creditors' meeting is as in 4.14.12 above.

4.30.16 Record of proceedings is similar to 4.14.13 above except that particulars not filed with court (but see also 4.31.5 below).

4.30.17 Other meetings of creditors:
At year's end : see 4.40 below
Final meeting: see 4.40 below

4.30.18 Section 98 does not prevent company from passing immediate resolution to wind up and then proceed to appoint a liquidator (by ordinary resolution) (see *Re Centrebind Ltd* [1967] 1 WLR 377), but in such circumstances liquidator's powers are limited until creditors meeting held. See 4.50 below.

4.31 Statement of affairs

4.31.1 Statement will include particulars of company's assets, debts and liabilities, names and addresses of creditors, their securities and dates given. Liquidator sends copy to registrar of companies within 7 days of meeting.

Director(s) liable to fine if, without reasonable excuse:

(1) fail to attend meeting

(2) fail to prepare statement of affairs

Reasonable and necessary expenses of preparing statement of affairs payable from assets. Creditors' meeting or liquidation committee to be informed of details.

s. 99

rr. 4.34, 4.38   [forms 4.18, 4.19, 4.20]

4.31.2   Where liquidator nominated by company prior to s. 98 meeting, directors deliver statement of affairs to liquidator forthwith upon its production.

r. 4.34A*

4.31.3   Within 28 days of s. 95 or s. 98 creditors' meeting liquidator must send report of meeting and copy or summary of statement of affairs to all creditors and contributories.

r. 4.49

4.31.4   Where liquidator who was formerly administrator discovers creditors not previously known to him he must send them a copy of his statement or report under rule 2.16 so noted.

s. 140

rr. 216, 4.49A*

4.31.5   At s. 98 meeting, if statement of affairs is not as at date of meeting directors must ensure that supplementary report of any material transactions after date of statement of affairs be given to the meeting (and that report recorded in the minutes).

r. 4.53B*

4.32   Submission of accounts

4.32.1   Applicable is 4.12.1 above, with necessary modifications.

4.32.2   With sanction of liquidation committee, if any, liquidator may make allowance out of assets for solicitor or accountant to assist person to prepare accounts.

rr. 4.40, 4.41

4.33 Procedure for proving debts

4.33.1 Liquidator invites creditor to submit claim (proof of debt) in writing.

[No prescribed form]

4.33.2 Liquidator to allow inspection of proofs, as in 4.15.4 above.

4.33.3 Admission and rejection of proofs for dividend, and appeal is as in 4.15.5 above.

4.33.4 Withdrawal or variation of proof is as in 4.15.6 above.

4.33.5 Expunging of proof by the court is as in 4.15.7 above.

4.34 Quantification of claims

As in 4.16 above.

4.35 Proof of secured creditors

Applicable is 4.17 above (with necessary modification to 4.17.1).

4.36 Appointment of liquidator

4.36.1 Procedure for appointment of liquidator is as in 4.18.1 except authority is s. 100 which is analagous to s. 139 but here director member or creditor may apply to court to settle dispute over appointment of liquidator; and except r. 4.63(2A) does not apply to CVL.
s. 100

4.36.2 Chairman certifies appointment upon receiving written statement of qualified insolvency practitioner who consents to act. Liquidator's appointment takes effect from passing of resolution for his appointment.
r. 4.101*   [forms 4.27, 4.28]

4.36.3 Where liquidator is appointed by court, under s. 100 (3) or s. 108:
(1) order not issued until liquidator files statement
(2) appointment effective from date of order
(3) liquidator sends notice of order to creditors and contributories within 28 days (or advertises if court so directs).
r. 4.103   [forms 4.29, 4.30]

4.36.4   Certificate (or order) is proof of appointment and authority.
         r. 4.105

4.36.5   Advertisement and registration of appointment is as in 4.18.5 above.

4.36.6   Upon appointment of liquidator, director's powers cease unless and
         to the extent liquidation committee or creditors sanction their
         continuance.
         s. 103

4.37   Appointment of liquidation committee

         (*NOTE*: the rules applying to liquidation committees in voluntary
         and compulsory liquidations are covered in 4.44 below).

4.37.1   The creditors may, at the first or any subsequent creditors' meeting,
         appoint a liquidation committee of at least 3 but not more than 5 of
         their number.
         s. 101(1)
         r. 4.152

4.37.2   Contributories may then appoint up to 5 members of committee but
         creditors may resolve to veto appointment of any or all contributory
         members (subject to contributories appeal to the court).
         s. 101 (2)

4.38   Vacation of office by liquidator

4.38.1   If a vacancy occurs by death, resignation or otherwise, the creditors
         may fill the vacancy. Continuing joint liquidator or any creditor can
         convene creditors' meeting for the purpose. Liquidator who ceases
         to be insolvency practitioner must vacate office.
         s. 104
         r. 101A*

         Resignation

4.38.2   Applicable are 4.19.1 above (except official receiver not notified)
         and 4.19.2 (grounds for resignation).

4.38.3   If creditors' meeting accepts resignation, liquidator sends notice to
         registrar of companies within 7 days. If new liquidator appointed,

chairman certificates such appointment, and new liquidator advertises his appointment as such.

s. 171(5)

rr. 4.110, 4.112   [form 4.33]

4.38.4 If creditors' meeting does not accept resignation, liquidator may apply to court for leave to resign.

r. 4.111   [forms 4.34, 4.35]

Removal of liquidator by creditors

4.38.5 Twenty-five per cent in value of creditors (excluding connected persons) may requisition meeting for removal of liquidator, and notice will state purpose of meeting. Creditor may apply to court to regulate, summon and conduct meeting.

Meeting may elect chairman other than liquidator, but if liquidator is chairman and resolution proposed for his removal, he may not adjourn meeting without consent of at least 50 per cent in value of creditors present, in person or proxy, and entitled to vote.

s. 171

r. 4.114   [form 4.22]

4.38.6 Chairman or new liquidator sends certificate of removal to registrar of companies.

r. 4.117   [form 4.38]

Removal of liquidator by court

4.38.7 See 4.19.8 above.

Release of resigning or removed liquidator

4.38.8 Applicable is 4.19.10 above.

4.38.9 Where creditors' meeting resolves against release (on resignation or removal) or upon removal by court, liquidator must apply to Secretary of State for his release. Secretary of State sends certificate of release to registrar of companies and copy to liquidator: effective date of release.

r. 4.122   [form 4.41]

Release on completion of administration

4.38.10 Liquidator calls final meeting of creditors on 28 days notice to all creditors who have proved. Creditors may question liquidator and resolve against his release, then liquidator applies to Secretary of State.

r. 4.126   [forms 4.22, 4.41]

4.38.11 Liquidator's duties on vacating office are as in 4.19.15 above.

4.38.12 At conclusion of winding up, liquidator sends final statement to registrar of companies. If winding up not completed 12 months after commencement, liquidator sends interim statement to registrar of companies and further statement every subsequent 6 months.

s. 192

r. 4.223*   [amended form 4.68]

4.39   Liquidator's remuneration

Applicable is 4.20 above.

4.40   Meetings

4.40.1 Meetings at each year's end are as in 4.28.1 above but meetings of creditors and contributories are called.

4.40.2 Final meeting prior to dissolution is as in 4.28.2 above but meetings of creditors and contributories are called.

4.41   Expenses of voluntary winding-up

All expenses properly incurred, including the remuneration of the liquidator, are payable out of assets in priority to all other claims.

See 4.48 below.

s.115

4.42   Conversion to winding up by the court

4.42.1 Where company is in voluntary liquidation, a winding-up petition may be presented by any of the persons mentioned in 4.2.1 above or by the official receiver, but the court shall not make a winding-up order unless it is satisifed that the voluntary winding up cannot be continued with due regard to the interests of the creditors or contributories.

s. 124(5)

4.42.2 Official receiver may apply to court for public examination of voluntary liquidator if irregularity is suspected.

s. 133(1)(b)

PROVISIONS APPLYING TO EVERY WINDING UP WHETHER
VOLUNTARY OR BY THE COURT

43 Setting aside transactions and solicitation

43.1 If liquidator enters into transaction with associate of his, any interested person may apply to court for order that transaction be set aside and liquidator compensate company for any loss suffered; unless:
(1) transaction had prior consent of court, or
(2) transaction for value and liquidator did not know person was associate of his
r. 4.149

43.2 If liquidator used improper solicitation to obtain proxies procuring his appointment, court may order he receive no remuneration, notwithstanding any contrary resolution of liquidation committee or creditors' meeting. A person making a corrupt inducement to affect the appointment of a liquidator is guilty of criminal offence.
s. 164
r. 4.150

44 The liquidation committee

44.1 A summary of the general principles is set out in 4.44.2 – 4.44.7 below. There are some differences in detail between the rules applying to voluntary and compulsory liquidations and in the latter between solvent and insolvent liquidations, as to the detail of which, the reader is referred to the Rules. See also 4.37 above (appointment of liquidation committee in voluntary liquidation) and 4.14.13 – 4.14.17 above (liquidation committee in compulsory liquidation and following administration).

44.2 Creditors and contributories may resolve to form committee and elect at least 3 members who agree to act. Creditors are eligible if they are entitled to vote at creditors' meetings. Committee comes into being when liquidator issues certificate of due constitution. Certificate is filed in court or sent to registrar of companies as appropriate, as is any amended certificate
rr. 4.151 – 4.154   [forms 4.47, 4.48, 4.49]

44.3 Liquidator's duty to report to committee on all material matters or on matters reasonably requested by the committee. Liquidator reports on progress of liquidation every 6 months or more frequently if requested. Members are entitled to inspect liquidator's records.
r. 4.155, 4.169

4.44.4 Meetings called by liquidator at his request or request of any credit member (within 21 days) or as specified by the committee. Liqui ator gives 7 days' written notice to each member (unless waived Quorum is 2 members or representatives. Representatives must ha written authority. Proxy or authorisation under C.A. s. 375 is to ᵗ treated as authority unless it contains statement to the contrary.
rr. 4.156–4.159*

4.44.5 Each member has one vote: resolution on simple majority. compulsory liquidation only the votes of creditor members count (resolution (unless only members are contributories). Resolutioᵣ recorded by liquidator. Postal resolutions may be agreed.
rr. 4.165 – 4.167

4.44.6 Members may resign; and membership automatically terminated member:
(1) becomes bankrupt (replaced by trustee)
(2) misses 3 consecutive meetings
(3) ceases to be creditor
Members may be removed by resolutions of relevant meeting creditors or contributories, upon 14 days' notice of resolutioᵣ Vacancies may be filled but need not be if liquidator and remainiᵣ members agree and total remaining not below 3.
rr. 4.160 – 4.163

4.44.7 Members' reasonable travel expenses are payable out of asseᵗ Transactions whereby members' representatives, associates or paᵣ members receive company's assets or profit from administration ᵣ permitted, except with leave of court or prior consent of committ if transaction for full value.
rr. 4.169, 4.170

4.44.8 The acts of the liquidation committee are valid notwithstandiᵣ any defect in the appointment, election or qualifcations of aᵣ committee member or representative or in the formalities of ᵢ establishment.
r. 4.172A

4.45 Distribution of assets

See chapter 11.

4.46 Disclaimer

4.46.1 Liquidator may, by giving prescribed notice, disclaim oneroᵂ property, notwithstanding that he has taken possession, endeavoured to sell or otherwise exercised rights of ownership in relation to it.

s.178(2)   [amended form 4.53]

46.2   Onerous property may be:
  (1) unprofitable contract
  (2) property which is unsaleable or not readily saleable or which may give rise to liability to pay money or perform onerous act
  s. 178(3)

46.3   Company's rights, interests and liabilities determine on date of disclaimer but do not affect the rights and liabilities of any other person.
  s. 178(4)

46.4   Notice of disclaimer fully identifying the property, with copy to be filed in court. Sealed and dated copy immediately returned to liquidator: effective date of disclaimer. Liquidator sends copy of notice to known interested person(s) within 7 days and forthwith to such persons subsequently discovered. Liquidator informs court, from time to time, of such notices given.
  rr. 4.187, 4.188   [amended form 4.53]

46.5   No time limit for exercising disclaimer but person interested in the property may apply in writing, requiring liquidator to decide whether he will disclaim or not. 'Notice to elect' must be delivered personally or by registered post. Liquidator must then disclaim (or not) within 28 days unless he applies to court for longer period.
  s. 178(5)
  r. 4.191   [form 4.54]

46.6   Liquidator may request of any person that he declare whether he has an interest in property, and details.
  r. 4.192   [form 4.55]

46.7   Disclaimer of leasehold property not effective unless copy served on any known underlessee or mortgagee and they had made no (successful) application to the court under s.181 (vesting order).
  s. 182
  r. 4.194

46.8   Any person who has interest in disclaimed property or who is subject to a continuing liability may apply to the court to vest the property in him. Application to be made within 3 months of knowledge of disclaimer. Submit affidavit in support stating:

(1)   nature and grounds of application
(2)   date he received notice of disclaimer (or became aware)
(3)   order sought
Seven days' notice to liquidator, with affidavit.
r. 4.194

4.46.9   Any person suffering loss because of disclaimer becomes creditor t
that extent. Any disclaimer is presumed valid and effective unles
liquidator has not complied with the Act or the Rules.
s. 178(6)
r. 4.193

4.47   Special manager

4.47.1   Where company in liquidation or provisional liquidator appointed
court may appoint any person to be special manager of company'
business or property. Applicant is liquidator (official receiver
liquidator or provisional liquidator) on grounds that special manage
necessary in view of:
(1)   nature of company's business or property
(2)   interests of creditors, contributories or members generally
Special manager need not be insolvency practitioner.
s. 177

4.47.2   Application to be supported by report setting out reasons and givin
estimate of value of (relevant) assets.
r. 4.206 (1) and (2)

4.47.3   Order may be made for a specific duration or until further order an
may be renewed. Court fixes remuneration and powers of specia
manager.
r. 4.206 (3) – (6)   [form 4.60]

4.47.4   Special manager must provide to the liquidator security equal to th
value of the (relevant) assets, whereupon liquidator files certificate o
adequacy in court. Cost of providing security is reimbursable from
assets (or by company if winding-up order not made).
r. 4.207   [No prescribed form]

4.47.5   Special manager must account to liquidator every 3 months.
r. 4.209

4.47.6   Appointment is terminated:
(1)   if winding-up petition dismissed or provisional liquidator dis
charged

(2) liquidator may apply to the court if appointment no longer expedient

(3) liquidator must apply to the court if creditors' meeting so resolves

r. 4.210

4.48 Order of payment of expenses out of assets

4.48.1 Liquidation expenses payable out of assets in the following order of priority:

(1) preserving, realising or getting in company's assets (official receiver liquidator)

(2) other expenses incurred by official receiver

(3) (a) official receiver's fee (s. 414)
    (b) repayment of deposit lodged by petitioner

(4) any other fees and remuneration payable to official receiver

(5) cost of security provided by provisional liquidator

(6) remuneration of provisional liquidator

(7) any deposit lodged on appointment of provisional liquidator

(8) petitioners' costs

(9) remuneration of special manager

(10) cost of assisting preparation of statement of affairs or accounts

(11) costs of application for release from obligation to submit statement of affairs or extension of time (by court order)

(12) necessary disbursements of liquidator including expenses of liquidation committee

(13) remuneration of any person employed by liquidator to perform services for the company

(14) remuneration of liquidator up to official receiver scale

(15) corporation tax payable on realisations

(16) balance of any remunerations due to liquidator

r. 4.218*

4.48.2 Where winding up by court immediately follows voluntary winding up, such costs and expenses of voluntary liquidation and remuneration of voluntary liquidator as court allows rank prior to 4.48.1(1) above.

r. 4.219

4.48.3 In a winding up by the court where assets are insufficient to meet liabilities the above priorities are subject to any contrary order of the court.

s. 156

r. 4.220

4.49   Restrictions on re-use of company name

4.49.1   A person who was a director or shadow director of a company at any
time in the 12 months prior to it going into insolvent liquidation,
must not, within 5 years of the date of liquidation, be involved in any
other company or business which uses the same or similar name or
trading style, without leave of the court under s. 216(3). Contraven-
tion is a criminal offence and such person may be personally liable
for any debts incurred by the new company during his involvement
with it.
ss. 216, 217

4.49.2   Where an application for leave is made the court may ask the
liquidator (or former liquidator) to report on the applicant's appar-
ent responsibility for that insolvency.
r. 4.227

4.49.3   Leave under s. 216(3) (see 4.49.1 above) is not necessary in the
following 3 situations:
   (1) Where a successor company acquires the whole, or substantially
        the whole, of the business of the insolvent company, under
        arrangements made by the liquidator (administrator, adminis-
        trative receiver or supervisor), the successor company may give
        notice under r. 4.228 to the insolvent company's creditor.
        Notice, to be given within 28 days of completion of arrange-
        ments, must specify:
           (a) name and number of insolvent company
           (b) circumstances of acquisition
           (c) name of successor company
        and may name the relevant person involved.
   (2) Where director or shadow director of the liquidating company
        applies to the court for leave within 7 days of date of liquidation
        he may so act without having such leave from the date of
        liquidation for 6 weeks or until the hearing of the application if
        earlier than 6 weeks.
   (3) Where person is involved in another company that has been
        known by a prohibited name throughout the relevant 12 months
        and has not been dormant during that time.
   rr. 4.228, 4.229*, 4.430

4.50   Liquidator's powers and duties

Voluntary winding up

4.50.1   Liquidator may, with sanction of the court or liquidation committee or creditors' meeting (sanction of extraordinary resolution in members' voluntary winding up), exercise the following powers:

(1) pay any class of creditors in full

(2) make compromise or arrangement with creditors or persons claiming to be creditors

(3) compromise, on agreed terms, all calls, debts, liabilities to and claims of the company; and take security to discharge such

Sched 4, Part I

4.50.2 The liquidator may, without sanction, exercise the following powers:

(1) bring or defend actions and proceedings in the name of the company

(2) carry on business of company so far as necessary for benefit of winding up

(3) sell company property as a whole or in parcels, by public auction or private treaty

(4) sign or execute receipts deeds etc in company's name

(5) prove and calim in bankruptcy or insolvency of contributory

(6) draw, accept, make or endorse any bill of exchange or promissory note in name of company

(7) raise money on security of company assets

(8) any act necessary to obtain money due from estate of contributory (including becoming personal representative)

(9) appoint agents

(10) do such other things as necessary for winding up company's affairs and distributing assets

Sched 4, Parts II and III

4.50.3 Additional powers:

(1) exercise court's power to settle list of contributories (see 4.21 above)

(2) exercise court's power of making calls (see 4.21 above)

s. 165(4)

4.50.4 Where liquidator disposes of company property to a connected person (s. 249) he must give notice to liquidation committee (if any). s. 165(6)

Creditors' voluntary winding up

4.50.5 Where liquidator is nominated by the company at general meeting (*Re Centrebind Ltd* [1967] 1 WLR 377), until convening of creditors' meeting (see 4.30 above) he may not exercise powers in 4.50.1–4.50.4 above, without leave of court. Liquidators powers, without leave, are:

(1) collect company property

(2) dispose of perishable goods or immediately wasting assets

(3) do such other things necessary to protect company's assets

s. 166

4.50.6 Liquidator must then attend creditors' meeting and report exercise of his powers. Liquidator must ensure that company and directors perform their obligations in calling creditors' meeting and preparing statement of affairs (see 4.30 and 4.31 above) or apply to the court for directions if default. Liquidator contravening s. 166 is liable to fine, and civil remedy under s. 212 and further sanctions under s. 133 and Part XIII of the Act.

s. 166

Winding up by the court

4.50.7 Liquidator's powers with sanction of court are as in 4.50.1 and 4.50.2(1) and (2) above.

Without sanction, the powers are as in 4.50.2(3)–(10) above.

s. 167

4.50.8 Exercise of all powers is subject to control of court and any creditor or contributory may apply to court in respect of exercise or proposed exercise of those powers. Also, any person who is aggrieved by act or decision of liquidator may apply to court for directions, as may liquidator in relation to any matter arising in winding up.

ss. 167, 168

4.51   Notification that company is in liquidation

Every invoice, order or business letter issued by or on behalf of company (liquidator or receiver or manager) must include statement that company is being wound up. In default, company and responsible officer is liable to fine.

s. 188

4.52   Interest on debts

4.52.1 Interest up to date of commencement of winding up, calculated at contract rate, is included in creditors' proof. Post-insolvency interest only payable if surplus after all creditors' claims paid in full, calculated according to contractual rate or court rate (at date of liquidation) and is payable pari passu to all creditors (see also 4.16.17 above).

s. 189

52.2 Liquidator can re-open a contract which is an extortionate credit
      transaction, and court may adjust contractual rate of interest (see
      8.11 below).
      s. 244

53 Courts general power to appoint or remove liquidator

If for any reason there is no liquidator acting, court may appoint a
liquidator. The court may, as cause shown (unfitness), remove a
liquidator and appoint another.
s. 108

54 Dissolution of companies after winding up

Voluntary winding up

54.1 Within one week of final meeting (in members' or creditors'
      voluntary winding up) liquidator sends final account and return to
      registrar of companies. Company is deemed dissolved 3 months after
      registration unless liquidator or any interested person obtains court
      order deferring date of dissolution.
      s. 201   [forms 4.71, 4.72]

Compulsory winding up

54.2 After final meeting, liquidator sends notice to registrar of companies
      or official receiver sends notice that winding up complete. Company
      dissolved 3 months after registration unless Secretary of State or any
      interested person obtains court order deferring date of dissolution.
      s. 205   [No prescribed form]

Early dissolution by official receiver

54.3 Where official receiver is liquidator, he may at any time, having
      given 28 days' notice of intention, to creditors and contributories
      and any administrative receiver, apply to registrar of companies for
      early dissolution if it appears that:
      (1) realisable assets insufficient to cover expenses of winding up;
           and
      (2) affairs of the company do not require further investigation.
      Company is dissolved 3 months after registration of application
      unless within that time Secretary of State gives contrary directions
      on application of official receiver or any interested person.
      s. 202   [No prescribed form]

4.55   Time limits

Where, by any provision of the Act or the Rules about winding up
the time for doing anything is limited, the court may extend the
time, either before or after it has expired, on such terms as it think
fit.

r. 4.3

5. Management Provisions Applying Where Company is Insolvent or in Liquidation

Contents

5.0 Introduction

Insolvency includes:
(1) approval of a voluntary arrangement
(2) making of an adminstration order
(3) appointment of administrative receiver

A company goes into liquidation when it passes a resolution for voluntary winding up or the court makes winding-up order

The office holder referred to in 5.3 – 5.7 includes official receiver whether or not he is liquidator.

s. 247

5.1 Public utilities

5.1.1 Office holder (administrator, adminstrative receiver, supervisor, liquidator or provisional liquidator) may request:
(1) public supply of gas
(2) supply of electricity by Electricity Board
(3) supply of water by statutory authority

(4) supply of telecommunication services by public telecommuni-
cations operator

Where the office holder makes such request after the effective date
(date of order, appointment or liquidation as appropriate), the
supplier may require office holder personally to guarantee payment
of charges for subsequent supplies but may not make it a condition
of supply that outstanding charges for previous supplies are paid (as
to which the supplier is usually an unsecured non-preferential
creditor).

s. 233

5.1.2   Parallel provisions apply in relation to individual insolvency.
s. 372

5.2   Getting in the company's property

(NOTE: not applicable to voluntary arrangements)

5.2.1   Where any person has possession or control of property, books,
papers or records to which the company appears to be entitled the
court may require that such property etc be paid or delivered etc to
the office holder (adminstrator, administrative receiver, liquidator,
provisional liquidator or official receiver).
s. 234(1)

5.2.2   Where the office holder seizes or disposes of property which is not
company property but at the time reasonably believed he was
entitled to do so, he is not liable for any resulting loss or damage
(unless caused by his own negligence) and he has a lien on the
property or proceeds of sale for his expenses incurred in the seizure
or disposal.
s. 234(3) and (4)

5.3   Duty to co-operate with office holder

(NOTE: not applicable to voluntary arrangements)

Office holder (administrator, administrative receiver, liquidator,
provisional liquidator or official receiver) may require information
form or attendance of any of the following:
(1) present of past officers of company
(2) anyone involved in company's formation if within one year
previous to effective date (date of order, appointment or
liquidation as appropriate)

(3) past or present employees (including under contract for services) within that previous year
(4) present or past officers or employees of another company which is or was within that year previous an officer of the company
(5) in the case of a company being wound up by the court, any person who was adminstrator, administrative receiver or liquidator

Non co-operation without reasonable excuse may result in fines.
s. 235

5.4 Private examinations

(*NOTE:* not applicable to voluntary arrangments)

5.4.1 Office holder (administrator, adminstrative receiver, liquidator, provisional liquidator or official receiver) may apply *ex parte* to the court for an order that the respondent:
(1) appear before court for examination
(2) answer interrogatories
(3) submit affidavit
(4) produce books papers or records
or any two or more of those purposes.

Application accompanied by statement of grounds. Order must be served personally and reasonable travel expenses tendered.
s. 236
rr.9.2, 9.3, 9.6   [form 9.1]

5.4.2 Respondent may be:
(1) any officer of the company
(2) any person believed to have property of the company or be indebted to it
(3) any person able to give information about the company, its formation, dealings, affairs or property

If respondent fails to appear or he has or may abscond, warrant may be issued for his arrest and seizure of books papers records money or goods in his possession.
s. 236

5.4.3 Record of examination, signed by respondent, may be used in evidence in later proceedings. Record of examination, affidavit or answers to interrogatories is not open to inspection, except to the applicant or other person who could have applied, without court order.
rr. 9.4, 9.5

5.4.4   Upon consideration of evidence obtained, court may order that any person deliver up property or discharge debt. Court may order that examination take place before another court in United Kingdom, or that respondent who is overseas be examined there.
s. 237

5.4.5   The rules (rr. 9.1–9.6) also apply to enquiry in bankruptcy under s. 366 (see 8.14 below.)

5.5   Extortionate credit transactions

(*Note*: applies to liquidation or administration)

Office holder (administrator, liquidator, provisional liquidator or official receiver may apply to the court to vary or set aside any credit transaction entered into by the company within 3 years of date of administration order or liquidation. A transaction is extortionate if the terms of it required grossly exhorbitant payments to be made for credit, or it otherwise contravened ordinary principles of fair dealing.
s. 244

5.6   Transactions at an undervalue

5.6.1   The administrator or liquidator may apply to the court where the company has at a relevant time entered into a transaction with any person at an undervalue.
s.238(1) and (2)

5.6.2   In the case of a transaction with a person connected with the company the relevant time is the 2 years prior to the insolvency.
s. 240 (1)(a)

5.6.3   Mere employment by the company is not a sufficient connection.
s. 240(1)(a)

5.6.4   In other cases the relevant time is the 6 months prior to the insolvency; and/or any time between the presentation of a petition for the making of an administration order and the order being made.
s. 240(1)(b) and (c)

5.6.5   The insolvency begins for these purposes when a petition is presented or on the date of commencement of the winding up.
s. 240(3)

5.6.6   At the relevant time the company must either be unable to pay its debts or become unable to pay them as a result of the transaction. s. 240(2)

5.6.7   A company enters into a transaction at an undervalue if:
(1) it makes a gift or receives no consideration for the transaction, or
(2) the consideration recovered is significantly less than the value in money or money's worth provided by the company
s.238(4)

5.6.8   There is a statutory defence if the transaction was entered into in good faith and there were reasonable grounds at the time for believing it would benefit the company.
s. 238(5)

5.6.9   The court in granting the application may make any order it sees fit to restore the position including the release or provision of security and the release or revival of guarantee obligations.
s. 238(3), 241

5.7 Preferences

5.7.1   The administrator or liquidator may apply to the court where the company has at a relevant time given a preference to any person. A preference is given if:
(1) the person is a creditor or guarantor for the debts of the company, and
(2) the company does anything which has the effect of improving the position of that person in the event of the insolvency of the company.
s.239

5.7.2   In the case of a transaction with a person connected with the company the relevant time is the 2 years prior to the insolvency.
s. 240(1)(a)

5.7.3   Mere employment by the company is not a sufficient connection.
s. 240(1)(a)

5.7.4   In other cases the relevant time is the 6 months prior to the insolvency; and/or any time between the presentation of a petition for the making of an administration order and the order being made.
s. 240(1)(b) and (c)

5.7.5   The insolvency begins for these purposes when a petition is presen-
        ted or on the date of commencement of the winding up.
        s. 240(3).

5.7.6   At the relevant time the company must either be unable to pay its
        debts or become unable to pay them as a result of the transaction.
        The court will only make an order if it is established that there was a
        desire to prefer the person concerned but such desire is presumed
        where the person preferred is connected with the company (other
        than as a mere employee). The presumption is rebuttable.
        ss.240(2), 239(5) and (6)

5.7.7   The court in granting the application may make any order it sees fit
        to restore the position, including the release or provision of security
        and the release or revival of guarantee obligations.
        ss. 238(3), 241

6. Voluntary Arrangements

6.0   Introduction

Voluntary arrangements following the insolvency of an individual parallel the voluntary arrangements for companies. A voluntary arrangement enables a debtor to reach a binding agreement with all his creditors. The debtor makes a proposal to a nominee, who must be an insolvency practitioner. The nominee reports to the court and summons a meeting of creditors where appropriate. If 75 per cent in value of the creditors agree the arrangement becomes binding on all persons who had notice of the meeting and were entitled to vote at it. A supervisor is appointed to oversee the arrangement. The supervisor may be the nominee or another insolvency practitioner. The Rules apply even if the debtor is an undischarged bankrupt (case 1) or if he is not (case 2). This procedure has proved popular with both debtors and creditors as in the right cases it offers a cheaper and more expedient alternative to bankruptcy.

6.1   Preparation and contents of debtor's proposal

6.1.1   Debtor prepares proposal for intended nominee to report to the court. Must contain:
(1) explanation why in debtor's opinion a voluntary arrangement is desirable and why creditors should agree
(2) details of assets with estimated values

(3) details of charges on assets
(4) the extent, if any, to which particular assets are to be exclude
(5) details of any assets not owned by the debtor which are to b
     included
(6) details of liabilities and how they are to be met of otherwis
     dealt with, referring specifically to:
     (*a*) preferential and secured creditors
     (*b*) treatment of any associates of the debtor who are creditors
     (*c*) (case 1 only) knowledge by the debtor of claims made unde
     ss. 339 (transactions at an undervalue), 340 (preferences), 34
     (extortionate credit transactions) or of circumstances giving ris
     to such claims and (case 2 only) whether such claims woul
     arise in the event of bankruptcy. There should be include
     details of how, if at all, the insolvent estate is to be indemnifie
     in respect of such claims.
(7) details of guarantees given of the debtor's debts by othe
     persons specifying which guarantors are associates of the debto
(8) proposed duration of arrangement
(9) proposed distributions (dates and amounts)
(10) remuneration and expenses of nominee and supervisor
(11) details of any guarantees or security to be given for arrangemen
(12) proposals as to inestment and banking of funds
(13) details of how funds unpaid to creditors on termination of th
     arrangement are to be dealt with
(14) proposals as to conduct of any business of the debtor
(15) details of any further credit applications and their repayment
(16) details of functions of supervisor
(17) name address and qualification of proposed supervisor
     r. 5.2, 5.3*   [No prescribed form]

6.1.2   With the written agreement of the nominee the proposal may b
        amended at any time up to delivery to the court of the nominee'
        report.
        r. 5.3(3)

6.2   Notice to intended nominee

6.2.1   Debtor gives notice of proposal in writing to intended nominee wit
        copy of proposal
        r. 5.4(1) and (2)   [No prescribed form]

6.2.2   Nominee agreeing to act endorses copy notice with date of receir
        and returns copy notice to debtor.
        r. 5.4(3) and (4)

6.2.3   In case 1 the debtor gives notice of his proposal to the official receiver and any trustee. This notice must contain the name and address of the insolvency practitioner who has agreed to act as nominee.
r. 5.4(5)   [No prescribed form]

6.3   Application for interim order

6.3.1   Debtor seeking moratorium may apply for interim order if he intends to make a proposal to his creditors for a voluntary arrangement.
ss. 252, 253   [new form 5.2]

6.3.2   While interim order is in force:
(1) no bankruptcy petition relating to the debtor may be presented or proceeded with
(2) no other proceedings and no execution or other legal process may be commenced or continued with against the debtor or his property except with leave of the court.
s. 252(2)

6.3.3   Application may be made:
(1) if debtor is undischarged bankrupt by the debtor himself, his trustee or the official receiver
(2) in any other case, by the debtor
s. 253

6.3.4   No application for an interim order may be made while a bankruptcy petition presented by the debtor is pending if the court has appointed an insolvency practitioner under s. 273 to enquire into the debtor's affairs and report.
s. 253(5)

6.3.5   While application for interim order is pending the court may stay any action, execution or other legal process against the property or person of the debtor. Any court in which proceedings are pending against a debtor who has made an application for an interim order may either stay the proceedings or allow them to continue on terms.
s. 254   [new form 5.1]

6.3.6   The court will only make an interim order if satisfied:
(1) that the debtor intends to make a proposal to creditors
(2) that on the day of making the application the debtor was an undischarged bankrupt or was able to petition for his own bankruptcy.

    (3) that the debtor had not in the previous 12 months applied for an interim order

    (4) that the nominee under the debtor's proposal is an insolvency practitioner and is willing and able to act

s. 255

6.3.7   An application for an interim order shall be supported by an affidavit of the following matters:

    (1) the reasons for the application

    (2) details of any execution or other legal process commenced against the debtor

    (3) that the debtor is either an undischarged bankrupt or able to petition for his own bankruptcy

    (4) the debtor has not applied for an interim order during the past 12 months

    (5) naming the nominee and stating that he is a person who is qualified to act as an insolvency practitioner in relation to the debtor, and is willing to act in relation to the proposal

A copy of the notice to the intended nominee endorsed with his agreement to act and also a copy of the debtor's proposal are exhibited to the affidavit.

r. 5.5(1) and (2)*   [No prescribed form]

6.3.8   On receipt by the court of the application and affidavit a date for the hearing is fixed. The applicant gives at least 2 days' notice of the hearing:

    (1) in case 1, to the bankrupt, the official receiver and the trustee (whichever is not the applicant)

    (2) in case 2, to any creditor who to the debtor's knowledge has presented a petition

    (3) in either case to the nominee

r. 5.5(3) and (4)   [No prescribed form]

6.3.9   Correct court for case 1 applications is that having conduct of bankruptcy (use same case number); for case 2 applications court is that where debtor could present own petition. Application must contain sufficient information to establish that it is brought in correct court.

r. 5.5A

6.3.10   Any of the persons given notice may attend or be represented at the hearing. If made, an interim order lasts for 14 days and the court fixes a venue for consideration of the nominee's report. The court

may extend the period to enable the nominee to have additional time
to prepare his report.
s. 256
r. 5.6   [new form 5.3]

5.3.11 Court seals 2 copies of order. Applicant serves one copy on nominee
and gives notice to all persons given notice of the application.
r. 5.7   [new form 5.2]

5.4   Statement of affairs

5.4.1   In case 1, if debtor has delivered a statement of affairs under s. 272
(debtor's petition) or s. 288 (creditors' petition) he need not deliver a
further one unless required to by the nominee for the purpose of
amplifying or supplementing the first one.
r. 5.8(1)

5.4.2   In case 2, the debtor shall within 7 days of delivery of proposal to
nominee (or within such extended time as he may allow) deliver to
nominee a statement of his affairs which must comprise:
(1) list of assets categorised for easy identification with estimated
     values
(2) particulars of secured claims
(3) names and addresses of and amounts due to preferential
     creditors
(4) names and addresses of an amounts due to unsecured creditors
(5) particulars of debts due to or from associates of the debtor
(6) such other particulars as the nominee may in writing require to
     be furnished for the purposes of making his report
r. 5.8(2) and (3)

5.4.3   Statement of affairs must not be made up to date earlier than 2 weeks
before date of notice to nominee. The nominee may allow an
extension of that period but shall give reasons. The statement shall
be certified by the debtor as correct to the best of his knowledge and
belief.
r. 5.8(4) and (5)

5.5   Nominee's report

5.5.1   If nominee decides he cannot prepare his report to the court on the
basis of the proposal and the statement of affairs he may require the
debtor to provide him with:
(1) further and better particulars as to why debtor is insolvent or
     threatened with insolvency

(2) particulars of any previous proposals made by him

(3) any further necessary information

The nominee may require the debtor to inform him if he has:

(a) been concerned in the affairs of any company anywhere which has become insolvent, or

(b) been adjudged bankrupt, or entered into an arrangement with his creditors.

s. 256

r. 5.9(1) and (2)   [No prescribed form]

6.5.2   To enable the nominee to prepare his report the debtor must give him access to his accounts and records.
r. 5.9(3)

6.5.3   Nominee must report to court not less than 2 days before any interim order ceases to have effect. Report must state:
(1) if nominee considers meeting of creditors should be summoned, and
(2) date time and place of any such meeting
r. 5.10   [No prescribed form]

6.5.4   Nominee must deliver to court with report:
(1) copy of proposal (with any authorised amendments)
(2) copy or summary of statement of affairs
r. 5.10(2)

6.5.5   If nominee indicates that a meeting of creditors should be summoned he shall annex his comments on the debtor's proposal to his report. Otherwise he shall give reasons for his opinion that there shall be no creditors' meeting.
r. 5.10(3)   [No prescribed form]

6.5.6   Court dates nominee's report. Any creditor may inspect.
r. 5.10(4)

6.5.7   In case 1, nominee shall send to the official receiver and (if any) the trustee:
(1) copy of debtor's proposal;
(2) copy of nominee's report and of his comments, if any
(3) copy or summary of the statement of affairs.
In case 2, the nominee shall send a copy of each of those documents to any person who has presented a bankruptcy petition against the debtor.
r. 5.10(5)*

6.5.8   If nominee fails to report on time, debtor may apply for his replacement to the court on 7 days' notice. Court may also continue or renew any interim order.

s. 256(3)

r. 5.11   [No prescribed form]

6.5.9   At the hearing to consider nominee's report any person given notice under r. 5.5(4) may appear or be represented. Rule 5.7 (6.3.10 above) applies to any order made at the hearing.

r. 5.12

6.6   Creditors' meeting

6.6.1   Where nominee has reported that meeting of debtor's creditors should be summoned, nominee proceeds to summon meeting to be held as proposed in report not less than 14 nor more than 28 days from consideration of report by court.

s. 257

r. 5.13(1)*

6.6.2   Nominee gives creditors at least 14 days' notice of meeting. Notice must specify court to which nominee's report delivered and state effect of rule on majority voting. With each notice must be sent:

(1)   copy proposal

(2)   copy statement of affairs (or summary)

(3)   nominee's comments on proposal

(4)   form of proxy

r. 5.13(2) and (3)   [No prescribed form of notice] proxy in Form 8.1

6.6.3   In fixing venue for meeting nominee shall have regard first to convenience of creditors. Meeting must be between 10 am and 4 pm on a business day.

r. 5.14

6.6.4   Nominee acts as meeting chairman but if unable to attend another insolvency practitioner may do so or an employee of the nominee or his firm who has insolvency experience.

r. 5.15

6.6.5   Chairman may not vote his proxies on questions of remuneration unless specifically directed.

r. 5.16

6.6.6   Every creditor given notice of meeting may vote. In case 1, votes are calculated on amount of debt as at the date of the bankruptcy order;

and in case 2, according to the amount of the debt as at the date of the meeting.
r. 5.17(1) and (2)

6.6.7   To pass the proposal or a modification of it requires a majority in excess of 75 per cent in value of creditors present and voting in person or by proxy. In respect of any other resolution majority must exceed 50 per cent in value.
s. 258
r. 5.18

6.6.8   If requisite majority for approval of the arrangement is not obtained chairman may, if so resolved, adjourn meeting and must notify court of adjournment.
s. 258

6.6.9   Adjourned meeting must be within 14 days. There may be more than one adjournment within that period. If proposal not then agreed it is rejected.
r. 5.19

6.7   Report of decisions to court

6.7.1   Chairman reports result of meeting to court and if meeting has not approved proposal court may discharge any interim order.
s. 259   [new form 5.4]

6.7.2   If meeting has approved proposal any bankruptcy proceedings stayed by interim order are deemed dismissed unless court otherwise orders.
s. 260   [new form 5.4]

6.7.3   Where debtor is undischarged bankrupt and arrangement is approved court may either annul bankruptcy order or give directions for purpose of facilitating the arrangement. Annulment will not take place within 28 days of date of report of meeting to court or if appeal pending.
s. 262   [new form 5.4]

6.8   Challenge of meeting's decisions

6.8.1   Application may be made to court by
(1)   the debtor
(2)   creditor entitled to vote
(3)   nominee
(4)   if debtor an undischarged bankrupt, his trustee or the official receiver

Alleging either or both:
(*a*) decision of meeting unfairly prejudices the interests of a creditor
(*b*) a material irregularity at or in relation to the meeting
s. 262 [No prescribed form]

5.8.2 Application must be made within 28 days of chairman's report to court of result of meeting.
s. 262(3)

5.8.3 Court may;
(1) revoke or suspend approval given by meeting
(2) direct summoning of further meeting to consider revised proposal
(3) give any consequential or supplemental directions
s. 262(4)

5.8.4 If court suspends or revokes approval, person applying for order serves sealed copies on the debtor, the supervisor and, in case 1, on the official receiver and the trustee.
r. 5.25(2)

5.8.5 If order includes direction for further meeting, notice is given to person required by it to summon meeting.
r. 5.25(3)

5.8.6 The debtor (in case 2) and the official receiver or the trustee (in case 1) forthwith give notice of order to all persons notified of meeting or who may be affected by order; and within 7 days they notify court whether they intend to make revised proposal or invite reconsideration of original proposal.
r. 5.25(4) [No prescribed form]

5.8.7 Person who applied for order gives written notice of it to Secretary of State within 7 days.
r. 5.25(5)

5.9 Implementation of arrangement

5.9.1 Forthwith after approval of the arrangement the debtor in case 2, and the official receiver or trustee in case 1, hand over possession of the assets included in the arrangement to the person appointed as supervisor.
s. 263
rr. 5.20, 5.21

6.9.2   In case 1, supervisor pays to official receiver or trustee any sums due
          by way of remuneration or for advances made in respect of the
          estate. Alternatively supervisor must give written undertaking to
          discharge same out of first realisation of assets.
          r. 5.21(2) and (3)

6.9.3   Chairman of meeting prepares report which shall:
          (1)   state whether the proposal was approved or rejected
          (2)   set out the resolutions taken and the decision on each
          (3)   list creditors with respective values and how each voted
          (4)   include any further information chairman considers appropriate
          r. 5.22(1) and (2)   [No prescribed form]

6.9.4   Chairman sends copy of report to the court within 4 days of the
          meeting. Immediately thereafter chairman gives notice of the result
          of the meeting to all those who were sent notice of it and in case 1
          the official receiver and any trustee.
          r. 5.22(3) and (4)*

6.9.5   Chairman reports to Secretary of State:
          (1)   name and address of debtor
          (2)   date of approval of arrangement
          (3)   name and address of supervisor
          (4)   the court in which chairman's report is filed
          rr. 5.23, 5.24   [No prescribed form]

6.9.6   Supervisor gives written notice of his appointment to Secretary of
          State who shall maintain register of reports, revocations, sus
          pensions and supervisor's accounts which shall be open to public
          inspection.
          r. 5.24(2)*   [No prescribed form]

6.9.7   If supervisor is to carry on business or trade in debtor's name, or
          realise assets or administer funds he is required to keep accounts.
          r. 5.26   [No prescribed form]

6.9.8   The approved arrangement binds every person who had notice of
          and was entitled to vote at the meeting. Where the debtor is an
          undischarged bankrupt the court may annul the bankruptcy order
          and/or give such directions as it thinks appropriate to assist imple
          mentation of the arrangement. The power to annul may not be
          exercised until after 28 days from the day on which the report of the
          meeting was made to the court or while an application to challenge
          the decision of the meeting is pending or there is an appeal pending
          or the time for appeal has not expired.
          ss. 260, 261

6.9.9 The court may make orders revoking or suspending the arrangement.
s. 262
r. 5.25*

6.9.10 The debtor or a creditor or any other person may apply to the court in respect of any act omission or decision of the supervisor and the court may give directions.
s. 263(3)   [No prescribed form]

6.10 Supervisor's accounts, reports and fees

6.10.1 Where accounts are required (see 6.8.7 above) then at least every 12 months supervisor must prepare receipts and payments account with progress report, to be sent to:
(1) the court
(2) the debtor
(3) all creditors bound by the arrangement
r. 5.26   [No prescribed form]

6.10.2 Court may on application of supervisor vary dates on which duty to report arises.
r. 5.26(5)

6.10.3 Secretary of State has power at any time to require supervisor to produce records accounts and reports either at supervisor's premises or elsewhere.
r. 5.27

6.10.4 The fees costs charges and expenses that may be incurred must be sanctioned by the arrangement or correspond to those which would be payable in bankruptcy. There may also be paid any disbursements of the nominee before approval of the arrangement and any remuneration as agreed with the debtor, his trustee or the official receiver.
r. 5.28

6.11 Completion of the arrangement

6.11.1 Within 28 days of final completion, supervisor gives notice of such to all creditors and to the debtor. With the notice is included a report detailing all receipts and payments and explaining any difference between actual implementation and proposal.
r. 5.29(1) and (2)

6.11.2 Copies of notice and report sent by supervisor to Secretary of State and the court.
r. 5.29(3)

6.11.3 Court may extend 28 day period.
r. 5.29(4)

7. Bankruptcy

Contents

7.0 Introduction

A creditor owed at least £750 (or a combination of creditors totalling at least that sum) may institute bankruptcy proceedings against a debtor. This is done by presenting to the court a bankruptcy petition. A debtor may present his own petition. The supervisor under a voluntary arrangement may petition and where a

90

criminal bankruptcy order has been made the petition is presented by the official petitioner or by any person specified in the order.

If the petition succeeds, a bankruptcy order is made. The individual is then adjudged bankrupt. His property passes into the hands of the official receiver or a trustee appointed by the creditors.

Where the debtor resides within the London insolvency district, the High Court has jurisdiction, otherwise application is made to the relevant county court with insolvency jurisdiction. The Lord Chancellor may by order designate those courts whose areas comprise the London insolvency district and those county courts which have jurisdiction.

A creditor wishing to petition must first have either served a statutory demand or have issued execution or other process on a judgment or order of the court which has been returned unsatisfied in whole or in part.

ss. 264, 268, 373 – 374
Powers of Criminal Courts Act 1973, s. 39(3)(b)

.1 Statutory demand

.1.1 Statutory demand is written demand served by a creditor on the debtor. The demand must specify whether it is for a debt payable immediately under s. 268(1) or not so payable (s. 268(2)) and must state:
(1) amount of debt and consideration/or other way it arises
(2) if made under s. 268(1) and founded on a judgment or order of a court, then details must be given of the judgment or order
(3) if made under s. 268(2), the grounds on which it is alleged that the debtor appears to have no reasonable prospect of paying the debt
(4) any other charge (including interest) and grounds
(5) the nature of any security held by the creditor and the value put upon it
(6) the purpose of the demand and an explanation that if it is not complied with bankruptcy proceedings may be commenced
(7) time limit for payment (at least 3 weeks)
(8) possible methods of compliance
(9) debtor's right to apply to the court to set aside the demand
(10) how to contact the creditor including details of one or more named individuals with authority to treat with the debtor including their addresses and telephone numbers

s. 268
rr. 6.1, 6.2   [new forms 6.1, 6.2 or 6.3]

.1.2 Statutory demand should be served personally if possible. If payment is due under a judgment or order and the creditor believes that

the debtor has absconded or is evading service and there is no rea
prospect of recovery of the debt by any other means the demand may
be advertised in one or more newspapers. Time for compliance then
runs from date of first advertisement.
r. 6.3

7.1.3   Within 18 days from date of service or advertisement the debtor may
apply to the court to set aside the demand. Time for compliance with
the demand then ceases to run. Debtor must support application
with affidavit which must exhibit a copy of the demand, specify the
date of service and state grounds on which debtor claims it should be
set aside.
r. 6.4   [forms 6.4, 6.5]

7.1.4   On receipt of debtor's application to set aside demand, court may
dismiss it without giving notice to creditor and time for compliance
starts running again. Otherwise court fixes venue and gives at least 7
days' notice to debtor or his solicitor, creditor and person named in
demand with authority to treat with debtor.
r. 6.5(1) and (2)

7.1.5   Court considers evidence on hearing and may summarily determine
the application or adjourn it and give directions.
r. 6.5(3)

7.1.6   Application may be granted if:
(1) debtor has counterclaim, set off or cross-demand equals or
exceeds claim against him, or
(2) debt is disputed on substantial grounds, or
(3) creditor is secured to an extent that value of security equals or
exceeds the debt, or
(4) court is satisfied on other grounds that demand ought to be set
aside
[form 6.6]

7.1.7   Court may require creditor to amend demand if security under-
valued but creditor may still present petition based on original
demand. If court dismisses debtor's application it shall authorise
creditor to present petition either forthwith or on or after a specified
date.
r. 6.5

7.2   Creditor's petition

7.2.1   Petition is presented to the High Court if:
(1) petitioner is minister of the Crown or a government department
and either the statutory demand specified that court or exe-

cution or other process following judgment has been returned
unsatisfied in whole or in part, or

(2) the debtor has resided or carried on business within the London
insolvency district for the greater part of the 6 months immediately preceding the presentation of the petition, or for a longer
period in those 6 months that in any other insolvency district,
or

(3) the debtor resides outside England and Wales, or

(4) the petitioner is unable to ascertain the residence of the debtor
or his place of business

r. 6.9(1)

7.2.2. In any other case petition is presented to the county court for the
insolvency district where the debtor has resided or carried on
business for the longest period during the 6 months immediately
prior thereto. If for the greater part of that period the debtor has
resided in the district of one court and carried on business in the
district of another, the petition shall be presented to the court in
which he has carried on business. If during that time he has carried
on business in more than one court the petition is presented to the
court where the debtor has had his principal place of business for the
longest time during those 6 months.

r. 6.9(3) – (4)

7.2.3 In any case where the debtor is subject to a voluntary arrangement
the correct court is that to which the nominee's report was
submitted.

r. 6.9(4A)*

7.2.4 The petition shall contain sufficient information to establish that it is
brought in the appropriate court.

r. 6.9(5)

7.2.5 The fee payable on filing the petition is £45 and a receipt for the
deposit payable (currently £240) must be produced on presentation.
Two copies of the petition are also required and are sealed by the
court. One sealed copy is for service on the debtor and the other is to
be exhibited to the affidavit verifying service. If the debtor is subject
to a voluntary arrangement a further copy of the petition must be
provided for sealing and service on the supervisor unless he is the
petitioner.

r. 6.10*   [forms 6.7, 6.8, 6.9 or 6.10]

7.2.6 Court endorses petition and sealed copies with date and time of
filing and fixes venue for hearing.

If the petition seeks the appointment as trustee of a supervisor then not less than 2 days before the hearing that person shall file in court a report including:

(1)   date creditors notified of supervisor's intention to seek appointment as trustee and

(2)   details of creditors' responses, including objections

r. 6.10(4) and (5)*

7.2.7   If petition based on statutory demand and there is serious possibility that debtor's property or the value of it may diminish within the 3 week period, the petition may be presented before that period has expired.

s. 270

7.2.8   Where the petition follows a statutory demand, an affidavit of service of each demand must be filed in court with the petition. The affidavit must exhibit a copy of the demand. If the demand has been served by advertisement the affidavit must be made by the creditor or a person having direct personal knowledge of the circumstances referred to in 7.1.2 above, the affidavit must also exhibit a copy of the advertisement.

r. 6.11*   [new form 6.11 or form 6.12]

7.2.9   On filing the petition the court arranges registration of it at the Land Registry and Land Charges Registry

r. 6.13   [form 6.13]

7.3   Verification of petition

7.3.1.   The petition must be verified by affidavit saying that the statements in it are true to the best of the deponent's knowledge, information and belief. The petition is exhibited to the affidavit. Where the petition is in respect of debts to different creditors each creditor's debts must be separately verified.

r. 6.12(1) – (3)   [form 6.13]

7.3.2   The affidavit must be made by:

(1)   the petitioner (or if there are two or more, any one of them), or

(2)   a director, company secretary or similar officer, or a solicitor who has been concerned in the matters giving rise to the petition, or

(3)   some responsible person who is duly authorised to make the affidavit and has knowledge of the circumstances.

r. 6.12(4)

7.3.3   If the affidavit is not made by the petitioner himself the maker must

identify himself in it and indicate his capacity and authority and his means of knowledge.
r. 6.12(5)

3.4 A petition based on a moneylending transaction made before 27 January 1980 shall at the hearing be supported also by an affidavit giving the particulars set out in s. 9(2) of the Moneylenders Act 1927
r. 6.20

3.5 If the petition is based on a statutory demand and more than 4 months have elapsed since service, the affidavit must give reasons for the delay.
r. 6.12(7)

4 Service of petition

4.1 A sealed copy of the petition is served personally on the debtor. If the court is satisfied on affidavit that the debtor is evading service it may order substituted service in such manner as it sees fit. Where a substituted service order is carried out the petition is deemed duly served on the debtor. If to the petitioner's knowledge a voluntary arrangement is in force a copy of the petition must be sent to the supervisor (unless he is the petitioner).
r. 6.14*   [forms 6.15, 6.16]

4.2 Service of the petition is proved by affidavit exhibiting a sealed copy of the petition and of any order for substituted service. The affidavit is filed immediately after service. If the debtor dies before service the court may order service on his personal representatives or on any other person it sees fit. The petition must be served at least 14 days before the hearing unless the court otherwise orders.
rr. 6.15, 6.18   [form 6.17 or 6.18]

5 The hearing

5.1 If the debtor intends to oppose the petition he shall at least 7 days before the hearing file in court a notice specifying the grounds of his objection, and send a copy of it to the petitioner or his solicitor.
r. 6.21   [form 6.19]

5.2 Any creditors may appear on the hearing of the petition and shall give notice to the petitioner specifying:
(1) the name, address, telephone number and any reference of the person giving notice or of his representative
(2) whether he supports or opposes the petition
(3) the amount and nature of his debt
The notice should be sent to arrive by 4 pm on the business day

before the hearing or any adjourned hearing. A creditor who fails t give notice may appear only with leave of the court.

r. 6.23   [form 6.20]

7.5.3   The petitioner prepares for the court a list of those creditors wh have given notice specifying their names and addresses, the respective solicitors (if known) and if supporting or opposing th petition.

r. 6.24   [form 6.21]

7.5.4   If, on the hearing, the court is satisfied that the statements in th petition are true, it may make a bankruptcy order. The court ma dismiss the petition if satisfied that the debtor is able to pay all h debts or secure or compound for them. A creditor seeking an orde on the basis that the debtor will be unable to pay a debt due at future date must satisfy the court that there has been a materi change in circumstances since the debtor incurred the liability.

s. 271

r. 6.25   [form 6.22]

7.5.5   If the petitioner fails to attend the hearing he may not prese another petition against the same debtor without leave of the cour

r. 6.26

7.5.6   If the petition has not been served and the petitioner requir another hearing date he must apply for another date giving reaso for non-service. If a new date is fixed the petitioner must notify ar creditor who has given notice of intention to appear.

r. 6.28

7.5.7   If the court adjourns the hearing, notice of adjournment and the ne date is given by the petitioner by post to the debtor and to ar creditor who has given notice of intention to appear.

r. 6.29   [forms 6.23, 6.24]

NOTE: the court always has power to extend time limits.

7.6   Substitution of petitioner

7.6.1   If a petitioner for any reason does not proceed with a petition consents to an adjournment of it the court may order that ar creditor appearing on the hearing be substituted as petition provided he wishes to prosecute the petition and is in a position present a petition himself e.g. if a creditor he has served a statuto demand and the time for payment has expired or he has unsucces fully attempted to levy execution.

r. 6.30   [new form 6.24A]

7.6.2 Any creditor may on the hearing apply for an order giving him carriage of the petition instead of the petitioner and without amendment of the petition. The court must be satisfied that the petitioner is either seeking the postponement or withdrawal of the petition or is not prosecuting the petition diligently. The court will not make a change of carriage order if the petitioner's debt has been paid, secured or compounded.
r. 6.31 [new form 6.24B]

7.7 Bankruptcy order on creditor's petition

7.7.1 A petition may not be withdrawn before the hearing. If the petitioner seeks withdrawal or dismissal on the hearing he must file an affidavit giving reasons, unless the court otherwise orders. If payment has been made or security given the affidavit must give particulars of the property sold or used.
r. 6.32 [form 6.22]

7.7.2 The bankruptcy order is settled by the court. It states the date of the presentation of the petition and the date and time of making of the order. It includes a notice requiring the bankrupt to attend on the official receiver.
r. 6.33 [form 6.25]

7.7.3 The order may include provision to stay any action or proceeding against the debtor.
r. 6.33(3)

7.7.4 Two sealed copies of the order are sent by the court to the official receiver who sends one to the bankrupt. The official receiver gives notice to the Chief Land Registrar and arranges for advertisement of the order in the Gazette and in such local paper as he sees fit.
r. 6.34 [new form 6.26]

7.8 Debtor's petition

7.8.1 A debtor may petition for his own bankruptcy on the ground that he is unable to pay his debts. The petition must state:
(1) debtor's name, address and any occupation and any other names he has used
(2) any names under which he carries on business and specifying any other persons with whom he carries on business
(3) the nature of his business and the business addresses
(4) any names under which he has carried on business during the period any of his debts were incurred and the addresses where he has resided or carried on business during that time

(5)   that the debtor is unable to pay his debts

(6)   particulars of any previous bankruptcy, composition or scheme of arrangement, voluntary arrangement or county court administration order during the previous 5 years

(7)   particulars of any current voluntary arrangement
s. 272
rr. 6.38, 6.39*   [form 6.27]

7.8.2   A statement of the debtor's affairs must be filed with the petition and be verified by affidavit. The statement must be in the prescribed form and contain all particulars required by that form (form 6.28)
r. 6.41

7.8.3   The petition is filed in the appropriate court (see 7.2.1, 7.2.2 and 7.2.3 above) with 3 copies. An additional 2 copies of the statement of affairs are required. The deposit payable is currently £120.
r. 6.40*

7.8.4   If the court does not hear the petition forthwith a venue is fixed. One copy of the petition is returned to the debtor with any venue endorsed. Another is sent to the official receiver if he is appointed interim receiver or a bankruptcy order is made. The third is sent to any insolvency practitioner appointed by the court. Where a voluntary arrangement is in force a venue is fixed and the supervisor is given at least 14 days' notice and may appear and be heard at the hearing. If the petition seeks the appointment as trustee of a supervisor then not less than 2 days before the hearing that person shall file in court a report including:

(1)   date creditors notified of supervisor's intention to seek appointment as trustee and

(2)   details of creditors' responses, including objections.
r. 6.42*

7.8.5   On filing the petition the court gives notice to the Chief Land Registrar for registration.
r. 6.43   [new form 6.14]

7.9   Appointment of insolvency practitioner by the court

7.9.1   If on the hearing of a debtor's petition it appears that:

(1)   the total unsecured debts are less than the small bankruptcies level (currently £20,000)

(2)   the value of the estate would be equal to or more than the minimum amount (currently £2,000)

(3)   during the past 5 years the debtor has not previously been bankrupt nor made a composition with his creditors nor a scheme of arrangement, and

(4) that it would be appropriate to appoint a person to prepare a report

then the court shall appoint an insolvency practitioner to prepare a report and to act as supervisor or trustee in any voluntary arrangement approved by a creditors' meeting.

s. 273(2)

.9.2 The court sends the practitioner a sealed copy of the order of appointment and copies of the petition and statement of affairs together with notice of the venue when the report will be considered. Notice of the venue is also given to the debtor. The practitioner files his report in court and sends copies to the debtor and to the official receiver to be received at least 3 days before the hearing. The debtor may attend the hearing and must do so if the court directs. He may be heard on the contents of the report.

r. 6.44*   [form 6.29]

.9.3. The practitioner appointed shall enquire into the debtor's affairs and report within the time specified by the court on whether the debtor is willing to make a proposal for a voluntary arrangement and if so stating whether a meeting of creditors should be summoned and if so when and where he proposes it should be held.

s. 274

.9.4 The court may make an interim order to facilitate the debtor's proposal (see 5.3 above) or may make a bankruptcy order.

s. 274(3)

.10 Bankruptcy order on debtor's petition

Similar to order on creditor's petition (see 7.7.2 – 7.7.4. above.

rr. 6.45, 6.46   [new forms 6.30, 6.26]

.11 Summary administration

.11.1 On a debtor's petition the court may issue a certificate for the summary administration of the bankrupt's estate if:

(1) the total unsecured debts are less than the small bankruptcies level (currently £20,000), and

(2) during the past 5 years the debtor has not previously been bankrupt nor made a composition with his creditors nor a scheme of arrangement

s. 275

r. 6.48   [new form 6.30]

.11.2 Any such certificate may be revoked if it later appears to the court that it ought not to have been issued. Either the court may do this of

its own motion or the official receiver may apply on 14 days' notice to
the bankrupt.

s.275(3)

r.6.50   [form 6.31]

7.12   Appointment of interim receiver

7.12.1 Any creditor, the debtor or an insolvency practitioner appointed
under s. 273(2) (see 7.9 above) may apply to the court to appoint an
interim receiver of some or all of the debtor's property. Application
may be made any time after presentation of a bankruptcy petition
and before making a bankruptcy order.

ss. 286, 287

r. 6.51   [No prescribed form]

7.12.2 The official receiver is usually appointed but where an insolvency
practitioner has been ordered to report under s. 273(2) the insolvency practitioner may be appointed.

s. 286(2)   [form 6.32]

7.12.3 The interim receiver's powers may be limited or restricted by the
court.

s. 286(3)

7.12.4 The applicant for an order appointing the official receiver will be
required by the court to pay to the official receiver a deposit to cover
his remuneration and expenses. The amount is determined by the
court and may be increased on application by the official receiver.

r. 6.53

7.12.5 The application must be supported by affidavit stating:
(1) the grounds
(2) whether or not the official receiver has been notified of the
application and supplied with a copy of it
(3) whether to the applicant's knowledge a voluntary arrangement
is in force
(4) the applicant's estimate of the value of the property or business
covered by the appointment
(5) If an insolvency practitioner has been apointed under s. 273(2)
and it is proposed to appoint him interim receiver, the fact that
he has consented to act

r. 6.51(2)   [No prescribed form]

7.12.6 Copies of the application and the affidavit must be sent to the
proposed interim receiver. If that person is the official receiver and
an insolvency practitioner has been appointed under s. 273(2) then

the practitioner must also be sent copies.
r. 6.51(4)

7.12.7 If the order is made, the court sends 2 sealed copies to the person appointed who sends one to the debtor.
r. 6.52(2)

7.12.8 The appointment terminates on the making of a bankruptcy order, the dismissal of the petition or the court so orders on the application of the debtor, any creditor, the interim receiver or the official receiver. On termination the court may give such directions as it sees fit. The remuneration of the interim receiver is paid out of the debtor's property.
rr. 6.56*, 6.57*

7.13 Petition on criminal bankruptcy order

If a court makes a criminal bankruptcy order the official petitioner or any other person authorised by the order may present a bankruptcy petition notwithstanding any pending appeal.
s. 264, 277

7.14 Petition following voluntary arrangement

The supervisor or any creditor bound by a voluntary arrangement may present a bankruptcy petition against a debtor but must prove that:
(1) the debtor has failed to comply with his obligations under the arrangement, or
(2) the debtor gave false or misleading information or there were material omissions in the debtor's documentation or statements made on his behalf, or
(3) the debtor has failed to co-operate
s. 264(1)(c), 276

7.15 Statement of affairs

7.15.1 Where a bankruptcy order has been made other than on a debtor's petition the bankrupt shall submit a statement of his affairs to the official receiver within 21 days. The statement shall be in the prescribed form (form 6.33) verified by affidavit and shall contain particulars of creditors, debts and other liabilities and his assets.
s. 288
rr. 6.58, 6.59

7.15.2   The official receiver supplies the bankrupt with the prescribed form
         and gives instructions on how to complete it.
         r. 6.60

7.15.3   The official receiver may release the bankrupt from his obligation to
         make a statement of affairs or may extend his time for doing so. The
         bankrupt may apply to the court if dissatisfied with the decision of
         the official receiver.
         s. 288(3)
         rr. 6.61, 6.62

7.15.4   The official receiver files the verified statement of affairs in court. If
         the official receiver thinks that the conduct of the bankruptcy would
         be prejudiced by disclosure of the statement of affairs, or any part
         of it, he may apply to the court for an order limiting its disclosure.
         r. 6.60, 6.61

7.15.5   If the bankrupt cannot himself prepare a proper statement of affairs
         he may apply to the official receiver to authorise payment out of the
         estate to some other person to assist in its preparation.
         r. 6.63

7.15.6   The official receiver may request the bankrupt to produce accounts
         for up to 3 years prior to presentation of the petition. The court may
         order production of accounts for any earlier period. The official
         receiver may require further information and that the accounts and
         information be verified by affidavit.
         s. 288
         rr. 6.58 – 6.66

7.15.7   Similar provisions apply to the provision of statement of affairs,
         accounts and information where the bankrupt filed his own petition
         (para 7.2 above).
         rr. 6.67 – 6.72   [Form 6.28]

7.16   Information to creditors

7.16.1   The official receiver has a general duty to report to creditors at least
         once after a bankruptcy order is made. Following the filing of the
         statement of affairs the official receiver shall send a summary to
         creditors with such observations as he considers appropriate. A copy
         is filed in court. If the official receiver has already reported to
         creditors he need only do so following filing of the statement of
         affairs if there are additional matters which he considers should be
         brought to the attention of creditors.
         r. 6.73*–6.75*

7.16.2   If the bankrupt has been released from his obligation to do a
         statement of affairs the official receiver shall send creditors a
         summary of the bankrupt's affairs so far as the official receiver
         knows them, together with any observations, unless he shall have
         done so before the bankrupt's release from the obligation to prepare
         a statement of affairs.
         r. 6.76

7.16.3   The court may, on the official receiver's application, relieve him of
         any duty to report, or authorise him to do so in a way other than
         required by the Rules; in considering any such application the court
         shall take into account the amount of funds in the estate.
         r. 6.77

7.17   **Creditors' meetings**

7.17.1   Following the making of a bankruptcy order if no certificate for
         summary administration has been issued the official receiver is under
         a duty during the 12 weeks after the making of the order to decide
         whether to summon a general meeting of the bankrupt's creditors.
         The purpose of the meeting is to apppoint a trustee of the bankrupt's
         estate. There is no such duty on the official receiver where:
         (1) the bankruptcy order was made on a petition presented follow-
              ing a criminal bankruptcy order, or
         (2) a request to summon a meeting supported by at least 25 per cent
              in value of the creditors has already been received, or
         (3) where the court has ordered that an insolvency practitioner who
              reported under s. 273 (7.9 above) shall be appointed trustee, or
         (4) where the court has appointed the supervisor of a voluntary
              arrangement as trustee

7.17.2   If the official receiver decides not to summon a meeting he shall
         within the 12 week period give notice to the court and to every
         identifiable creditor. Upon giving such notice the official receiver
         becomes trustee.
         s. 293 (2) and (3)

7.17.3   If there is no certificate for summary administration in force and if
         the official receiver has not yet decided to summon a creditors'
         meeting, or has decided not to summon one, any creditor may
         request the official receiver to summon a meeting. If the request is
         supported by at least 25 per cent in value of the creditors (including

the one making the request) the official receiver shall summon th
requested meeting.
s. 294
rr. 6.79, 6.83   [form 6.34]

7.17.4 Where the official receiver decides to summon a meeting (7.17.
above) he shall fix a venue for the meeting not more than 4 month
from the date of the bankruptcy order. Notice of the meeting i
given to the court forthwith and at least 21 days prior thereto t
every identifiable creditor. The notice given to creditors mus
specify a time and date not more than 4 days before the meeting b
which proofs of debt and any proxies must be lodged. Notice of th
meeting must also be given by public advertisement.
r. 6.79(1) – (5)

7.17.5 Where the official receiver has been requested to summon a meetin
(7.17.3 above) he shall withdraw any notice given that he ha
decided not to summon a meeting (7.17.2 above); fix the venue o
the meeting for within 3 months of receipt of the creditor's request
and proceed as if he had decided to summon a meeting (7.17.
above).
r. 6.79(6)

7.17.6 The meeting is known as the first meeting of creditors. The onl
resolutions taken shall be:
(1) to appoint a trustee (or joint trustees)
(2) to establish a creditors' committee
(3) if it is resolved not to establish a committee, to fix th
remuneration of the trustee or to defer consideration of same
(4) if 2 or more persons are appointed trustee, to specify whethe
they are to act by only one or jointly
(5) whether the meeting was requisitioned, a resolution authorisin
payment out of the estate of the cost of summoning and holdin
the meeting
(6) to adjourn for not more than 3 weeks
(7) any other resolutions which chairman may allow for specia
reasons
r. 6.80

7.17.7 The official receiver or the trustee may at any time summor
meetings of creditors to ascertain their wishes. At least 21 days
notice must be given. Notice must specify time and date not mor
than 4 days before meeting by when proxies (and proofs by thos
who have not already done so) must be lodged. Notice may also be
given by advertisements and court may so direct.
r. 6.81   [form 6.35]

7.17.8 Official receiver is chairman of meeting convened by him or he may nominate some other person to be chairman. If nominee is not another official receiver or a deputy official receiver the nomination must be in writing. Where meeting is convened by person other than official receiver that person or his nominee shall be chairman. Nominee must be insolvency practitioner or an experienced employee of the trustee or his firm. The nomination must be in writing.
r. 6.82

7.17.9 Any request by creditors to the official receiver or trustee to summon a meeting shall be accompanied by:
(1) list of concurring creditors showing value
(2) written confirmation of their concurrence
(3) statement of purpose of proposed meeting
Request must have concurrence of 25 per cent in value – (1) and (2) above not necessary if requisitioning creditor's debt is alone sufficient.
    Meeting is fixed to take place within 35 days on 21 days notice.
r. 6.83   [form 6.34]

7.17.10 Notice of all meetings must be given to bankrupt. If he does not attend he must be given notice of any adjournment. Bankrupt may be required to attend but may not otherwise do so except at discretion of chairman. Such questions may be put to the bankrupt as the chairman may allow.
r. 6.84   [form 6.36]

7.17.11 The court may order that notice of any meeting be given by advertisement only.
r. 6.85

7.17.12 Meetings are to be held between 10 am and 4 pm on business day at venue convenient to persons invited. Proxy forms are to be sent with notices (form 8.5).
r. 6.86

7.17.13 Persons seeking meeting (other than official receiver or trustee) must deposit security for expense of meeting but resolution may be passed that expenses be payable out of the estate.
r. 6.87

7.17.14 Chairman makes and keeps minutes of meeting attendance list and records of resolutions and files particulars of resolutions with court.
r. 6.95

7.18   Voting

7.18.1   Resolution is passed by majority in value of votes cast in person or by proxy. Where resolution is for the appointment of a trustee:
  (1)   if there are 2 nominees the person who obtains most support is appointed
  (2)   if 3 or more nominees and one has a clear majority over both or all the others together, that one is appointed
  (3)   in any other case, votes shall continue to be taken disregarding at each vote any nominee who has withdrawn or who obtained least support last time until a clear majority is obtained for any one nominee
  r. 6.88

7.18.2   Creditor may only vote if he has lodged proof of debt as required and it has been admitted for voting purposes and any requisite proxy has been lodged.
  r. 6.93

7.18.3   Votes calculated according to creditor's debt which should be for liquidated sum except chairman may estimate minimum entitlement. Secured creditor can vote only on balance of debt after deducting value of security estimated by him.
  rr. 6.93 – 6.94

7.18.4   Chairman has power at any meeting to admit or reject a creditor's proof for voting purposes and if in doubt may mark it as objected to. Aggrieved creditor may appeal to court who may order another meeting to be summoned. Chairman not liable in costs unless court orders.
  r. 6.94

7.19   Proofs of debt

7.19.1   Creditor wishing to recover debt must submit written proof of debt in proper form to official receiver or trustee (Crown may use other form). The trustee may require a claim to be verified by affidavit.
  rr. 6.96   [forms 6.37, 6.38, 6.39]

7.19.2 Official receiver or trustee sends forms of proof to all known creditors with his first notice to creditors.
r. 6.97*

7.19.3 Proof of debt will state:
(1) creditor's name and address
(2) amount of claim at date of bankruptcy order
(3) whether interest included
(4) whether VAT included
(5) whether any part is preferential
(6) how and when debt incurred
(7) details of any security
(8) name, address and authority of signatory
Proof should refer to any documents which substantiate debt. Documents need not be attached to proof but must be produced if required. Cost of proving is borne by creditor, but court may otherwise order.
rr. 6.98 – 6.100

7.19.4 Trustee will allow inspection of proofs by:
(1) any creditor who has proved unless proof rejected
(2) the bankrupt
(3) any person acting for either of the above
r. 6.101

7.19.5 A moneylender's proof in respect of a transaction made before 27 January 1980 shall have endorsed or annexed to it a statement detailing the matters mentioned in s. 9(2) of the Moneylenders Act 1927.
r. 6.102

7.19.6 If trustee rejects proof in whole or in part he sends written statement of reasons to creditor who may apply to the court within 21 days if dissatisfied with decision. Bankrupt or any other creditor may also apply to court in respect of trustee's decision to admit or reject any proof. Time for that application is 21 days from becoming aware of decision. Court fixes venue and applicant gives notice to trustee and to creditor, if not himself. Trustee files with court the relevant proof and a copy of his statement of rejection.
r. 6.104   [No prescribed form of application]

7.19.7 Creditor may at any time withdraw or vary proof with agreement of trustee.
r. 6.106

7.19.8   Trustee or any creditor may apply to court if he thinks a proof has
         been wrongly admitted or ought to be reduced.
         r. 6.107   [No prescribed form]

7.19.9   Creditor holding negotiable instrument must produce it or certified
         copy upon request.
         r. 6.108

7.19.10 Trustee deducts any proper discounts that the bankrupt would have
         been entitled to, except those for immediate early or cash settlement.
         r. 6.110

7.19.11 Foreign currency debts are converted into sterling at the official
         exchange rate at the date of order.
         r. 6.111

7.19.12 Rent or other periodical payments are calculated to date of order.
         r. 6.112

7.19.13 Interest-bearing dates are calculated to date of order (interest not
         previously reserved or agreed may be payable in certain cir-
         cumstances).
         r. 6.113*

7.19.14 Future debts may be proved subject to adjustment if dividend paid
         before due date.
         r. 6.114

7.20   Secured creditors

7.20.1   Secured creditor estimates value of his security at date of order and
         may revise his estimate with agreement of trustee or leave of the
         court. But if he was petitioner and has valued security in petition or
         has voted on unsecured balance can only re-value with leave of court.
         r. 6.115

7.20.2   If secured creditor does not disclose his security in his proof,
         security is surrendered (may apply to court for relief if honest
         mistake).
         r. 6.116

7.20.3   Trustee may redeem security at value stated in proof on 28 days'
         notice to secured creditor who may within 21 days seek to re-value
         (see 7.20.1 above).
         r. 6.117

7.20.4 If trustee does not accept secured creditor's estimate of value he may test it by offering property for sale.
r. 6.118

7.20.5 If creditor realises his security, the net amount realised shall be substituted for the value previously put upon the security.
r. 6.119

7.21 Appointment of trustee

7.21.1 Where person appointed trustee by creditor's meeting, the chairman certifies the appointment when provided with written statement by appointee that he is an insolvency practitioner and consents to act. The chairman (if not the official receiver) sends the certificate to the official receiver. A copy is filed in court and the appointment becomes effective on the date the appointment is certified. The certificate, endorsed with the date of filing, shall be sent by the official receiver to the trustee.
r. 6.120   [form 6.40 or 6.41]

7.21.2 Where a trustee is appointed by the court under s. 297(3), (4) or (5) the order of the court shall not issue until the appointee has filed a statement that he is an insolvency practitioner and consents to act. The court sends 2 copies of the order to the official receiver who sends one to the trustee whose appointment takes effect from the date of the order.
r. 6.121   [form 6.42 or 6.43]

7.21.3 If no trustee is appointed by a creditors' meeting, the official receiver has a duty to decide whether to refer the need for an appointment to the Secretary of State who shall either make an appointment or decline to do so.
s. 295, 296
r. 6.122

7.21.4 If for any reason there is a vacancy in the office of trustee the official receiver may refer the need for an appointment to the Secretary of State who shall either make an appointment or decline to do so.
s. 300
r. 6.122

7.21.5 If the Secretary of State makes an appointment he shall send 2 copies of the certificate of appointment to the official receiver who shall send one to the trustee and file the other in court.
r. 6.122(2)

7.21.6   A sealed copy of the trustee's order or certificate of appointment is
         proof of his authority.
         r. 6.123

7.21.7   If a trustee is appointed by creditors' meeting he shall on receipt of
         his certificate give notice in such newspaper as he thinks appropriate
         for ensuring it comes to the notice of creditors.
         r. 6.124

7.21.8   When the appointment takes effect the official receiver shall put the
         trustee into prossession of the estate.
         r. 6.125

7.22   Vacation of office by trustee

7.22.1   A trustee may resign because:
         (1) of ill health, or
         (2) he intends to cease to practice as an insolvency practitioner, or
         (3) there is some conflict of interest or change of personal circum-
              stances which makes it impracticable for him to cotinue, or
         (4) if he is a joint trustee, he and the other(s) agree it is no longer
              expedient to have the same number of joint trustees
         s. 298

7.22.2   The resigning trustee must call a meeting of creditors, notice of
         which must be given to the official receiver. The notice of meeting
         must be accompanied by an account of the trustee's administration,
         including a summary of his receipts and payments and a statement
         that he has reconciled his account with that held by the Secretary of
         State. If no quorum is present at the meeting it is deemed to have
         been held and the resolutions for remuneration and resignation
         passed.
         r. 6.126*

7.22.3   If the meeting accepts the trustee's resignation the chairman sends
         the official receiver a certificate to that effect. If a new trustee is
         appointed the procedure at 7.21.1 above is followed. If the meeting
         refuses to accept the trustee's resignation he may apply to the court.
         r. 6.127   [form 6.44]

7.22.4   A meeting of creditors may be summoned to remove the trustee. The
         notice convening the meeting shall state that this is the purpose, or
         one of the purposes of the meeting; and a copy is sent to the official
         receiver. At the meeting a chairman other than the trustee or his
         nominee may be elected. A new trustee may be appointed. A

creditor may apply to the court for directions as to the conduct of such meeting.

r. 6.129   [form 6.35]

22.5 Application may be made to the court for removal of a trustee. The court may dismiss the application but only if the applicant has had an opportunity to be heard *ex parte*. If the application is not then dismissed the court shall fix a venue for the hearing. At least 14 days before the hearing the applicant shall send to the trustee and the official receiver notice of it, together with a copy of the application and of any supporting evidence.

r. 6.132   [form 6.48]

22.6 The Secretary of State may decide to remove a trustee but shall first give the trustee and the official receiver notice of his decision and the grounds of it and specify a period within which the trustee may make representations.

r. 6.133

22.7 When advertising his appointment the new trustee shall state that his predecessor has resigned or been removed and (if it be so) that he has been given his release.

r. 6.134

23   Release of trustee and remuneration

23.1 Where a trustee's resignation has been accepted by a meeting of creditors which has not resolved against his release he is released on the date his resignation becomes effective.

r. 6.135(1)

23.2 Where creditors have voted against his release or he has been removed the trustee shall apply to the Secretary of State for his release.

r. 6.135(3)   [form 6.49]

23.3 Where the official receiver is replaced by another trustee, the official receiver is released either when he gives notice to the court that he has been replaced or, where the new trustee is appointed by the court, at such time as the court may determine.

s. 299

r. 6.136

7.23.4 If the official receiver while he is the trustee gives notice to the Secretary of State that the administration is complete, the date of his release shall be determined by the Secretary of State. Before giving such notice the official receiver shall notify creditors and the bankrupt of his intention and send them a summary of his receipts and payments.
ss. 299, 300

7.23.5 Where the trustee is not the official receiver he must give at least 28 days' notice to creditors and the bankrupt of the final meeting. The trustee shall report to the meeting his administration of the estate including a summary of his receipts and payments and a statement that he has reconciled his account with that held by the Secretary of State. The meeting shall determine whether the trustee shall have his release. The trustee should retain a sufficient sum from the estate to cover the cost of the final meeting.
ss. 299, 300

7.23.6 The creditors may question the trustee and may resolve against his release. If they do the trustee may apply for his release to the Secretary of State. The trustee gives notice to the court of the holding of the final meeting stating whether or not he was given his release. If there is not quorum present at the final meeting it is deemed to have been held, and the creditors not to have resolved against release.
r. 137   [form 6.50]

7.23.7 The trustee's remuneration is fixed either as a percentage of assets realised or distributed or both, or by reference to the time spent by the trustee and his staff.
r. 6.138(2)

7.23.8 Where the official receiver is not the trustee the remuneration is fixed by the creditors' committee. If there is no committee it may be fixed by the creditors.
r. 6.138(3) and (4)

7.23.9 If the remuneration is not fixed as above it shall be on the scale laid down for the official receiver by general regulations.
r. 6.138(6)

7.23.10 Joint trustees should agree between themselves an apportionment of remuneration. Any dispute may be referred either to the creditors' committee, the creditors or the court.
r. 6.139(2)

7.23.11 If the trustee is dissatisfied with the remuneration fixed by the creditors' committee he may request it to be increased by resolution of the creditors.
r. 6.140

7.23.12 The trustee is entitled in any event to have final recourse to the court to determine his remuneration but the creditors may be represented. The costs will usually be borne by the estate.

Any creditor may with the concurrence of at least 25 per cent in value of creditors (including himself) apply to the court in any case to have the trustee's remuneration reduced on the ground that it is excessive. The creditor will usually have to pay the costs unless the court orders otherwise.
r. 6.141*, 6.142   [No prescribed form]

7.24   Creditors' committee

7.24.1 Any meeting of creditors where the official receiver is not the trustee may establish a creditors' committee of at least 3 and not more than 5 creditors. A body corporate may be a committee member but can act only through its authorised representative.
ss. 301 – 303
r. 6.150

7.24.2 The committee comes into being only when the trustee has issued a certificate of due constitution.
r. 6.151 (1)   [form 6.52]

7.24.3 The trustee issues the certificate when at least 3 of the nominated members have agreed to act. Agreement may be given by a proxy holder. As and when any other members signify their agreement the trustee shall issue an amended certificate.
r. 6.151 (3)* and (4)*   [form 6.52]

7.24.4 The certificate and any amended certificates shall be filed in court by the trustee. Any change in membership of the committee must be reported by the trustee to the court.
r. 6.151 (5) and (6)   [form 6.53]

7.24.5 The trustee should report to the committee all matters which appear to be of concern to them, but the trustee need not respond to frivolous or unreasonable requests for information or where the cost of doing so would be excessive or the estate is without sufficient funds to enable him to comply.
r. 6.152

7.24.6   The trustee determines the venue for meetings of the committee. Th
         first meeting should take place within 3 months of the trustee'
         appointment or, if later, the establishment of the committee. A
         committee member may request a meeting. The chairman at meet
         ings shall be the trustee or a person nominated by him who shall b
         an insolvency practitioner or an experienced member of the trustee'
         staff.
         rr. 6.153, 6.154

7.24.7   The quorum for a committee meeting is 2 members provided a
         have been given at least 7 days' notice of the meeting or have waive
         notice.
         r. 6.155

7.24.8   A member of the committee may be represented by another perso
         holding his written authority or by his proxy holder but not by:
         (1)   another committee member
         (2)   a body corporate
         (3)   an undischarged bankrupt
         No person may represent more than one committee member at th
         same meeting.
         r. 6.156*

7.24.9   A committee member may resign by written notice to the trustee
         Membership of the committee is automatically terminated if:
         (1)   a member becomes bankrupt (he is replaced by his trustee), o
         (2)   he misses 3 consecutive meetings (unless it is otherwise resolve
               at the third meeting), or
         (3)   he ceases to be a creditor
         rr. 6.157, 6.158

7.24.10 A creditors' meeting may vote to remove a committee member
         Vacancies need not be filled if the trustee and a majority of th
         remaining committee so agree; otherwise they may be filled b
         resolution of the committee or a creditors' meeting.
         rr. 6.159, 6.160

7.24.11 Each committee member has one vote and resolutions are passed b
         simple majority. The trustee may obtain resolutions by post but
         member may require a meeting.
         r. 6.161, 6.162*

7.24.12 The trustee may be required by the committee to report in writing t
         each member but not more than once in any 2 month period.
         r. 6.163   [No prescribed form]

7.24.13 Travelling expenses incurred by the committee members shall be paid by the trustee out of the estate.
r. 6.164

7.24.14 A committee member shall not enter into transactions with the estate involving any payment to him or acquire any asset out of the estate without the prior leave of the court or prior sanction of the committee.
r. 6.165

7.24.15 Where there is no committee or where the official receiver is trustee, the functions of the committee shall be carried out by the Secretary of State
r. 6.166

7.24.16 The bankrupt or any creditor or anyone else dissatisfied with the actions of a trustee may apply to the court. The trustee may himself apply to the court for directions in relation to any matter arising under the bankruptcy.
s. 303

7.25   Discharge of bankrupt

7.25.1 First-time bankrupts obtain automatic discharge after 3 years, shortened to 2 years where a certificate for summary administration of the estate has been issued.

7.25.2 Where a bankrupt has previously been bankrupt within 15 years of the subsequent bankruptcy order, he must apply to the court for discharge and may do so after 5 years.

7.25.3 The court may on the application of the official receiver suspend the automatic discharge provisions where the bankrupt has failed to comply with his obligations.

7.25.4 The automatic discharge provisions do not apply where the bankruptcy adjudication followed a criminal bankruptcy order.

7.25.5 The court may impose conditions relating to future income and property when granting an application for discharge
ss. 279, 280
rr. 6.215 – 6.223   [forms 6.72 – 6.77]

7.26   Annulment of bankruptcy order

7.26.1 The court has power to annul a bankruptcy order at any time and
even after discharge on grounds that either:
(1) the order ought not to have been made, or
(2) the debts and expenses of the bankruptcy have all been paid or
secured for

7.26.2 The official receiver and any trustee must be given in the case of an
application under (1) above notice in sufficient time to enable them
to attend the hearing and if under (2) above at least 28 days notice of
the hearing of the application and copies of the supporting affidavit
evidence.
s. 282
rr. 6.206*–6.214   [form 6.71]

8. Protection of Bankrupt's Estate and Investigation

Contents

8.0 Introduction

This chapter contains brief notes on the more common procedures available to the trustee to realise the bankrupt's estate and investigate his financial affairs.

8.1 Special manager

8.1.1 The court may appoint a special manager of the bankrupt's estate or business, or of the property or business of a debtor in whose case an interim receiver has been appointed under s. 286.
s. 370(1)   [form 6.54]

8.1.2   The application may be made by the official receiver or the trustee in any case where it appears necessary. The application must be supported by a report giving reasons.
s. 370(2)
r. 167

8.1.3   The special manager must give security of not less than the value of the estate, property or business he is to manage.
s. 370(5)
rr. 6.168 – 6.171

8.2   Public examination

8.2.1   After the making of a bankruptcy order, and at any time before discharge, the official receiver may apply to the court for the public examination of the bankrupt. The court is obliged to grant the application and shall appoint a venue for the hearing.
s. 290(1) and (2)
r. 172(1) and (2)   [new form 6.55]

8.2.2   The official receiver gives at least 14 days' notice of the hearing to any trustee, special manager and every identifiable creditor. The official receiver may advertise notice of the order in one or more newspaper.
r. 172(3) and (4)

8.2.3   Any creditor may request the official receiver to apply for a public examination in writing and with the written concurrence of at least 50 per cent in value of the creditors. The request shall state the reasons why it is made. A single creditor whose debt is sufficient may make the request.
s. 290(2)
r. 6.173 (1)   [form 6.56]

8.2.4   The official receiver may apply to the court to relieve him from making the application if he thinks the request of the creditors is unreasonable. A deposit must be given by the requesting creditor of a sum sufficient to cover the cost of the examination.
r. 6.173(2) and (4)

8.2.5   The following may take part in the examination and question the bankrupt concerning his affairs, dealings and property and the causes of his failure:

(1) the official receiver, and in criminal bankruptcy the official petitioner
(2) the trustee, if his appointment has taken effect.
(3) any special manager.
(4) any creditor who has tendered a proof of debt

A written record is taken of the examination. The bankrupt may be represented by solicitor or counsel at his own expense.

s. 290(4)
r. 6.175   [form 6.58]

8.2.6   Where creditors have requested a public examination the court may order the cost of it to be paid out of the deposit.
r. 6.177

8.3   Disclaimer by trustee

8.3.1   The trustee may by notice disclaim any onerous property. Disclaimer releases the bankrupt, his estate and the trustee from any liability in respect of the property disclaimed but does not affect the rights or liabilities of any other person. A person affected may apply for a vesting order if appropriate.

8.3.2   The notice should contain particulars of the property and be signed by the trustee. The notice is filed in court with a copy, which is sealed and returned to the trustee. Within 7 days of the return of the notice to him the trustee shall send or give copies of the notice to every person affected.

8.3.3   The trustee requires the leave of the court before he may disclaim after-acquired property (s. 307) or personal property of the bankrupt exceeding reasonable replacement value (s. 308)

8.3.4   The trustee may not disclaim property where he has failed within 28 days to respond to a notice requiring him to decide whether he will disclaim or not.

8.3.5   Any person affected by disclaimer who suffers loss or damage may prove in the bankruptcy.
ss. 315 – 321
rr. 6.178 – 6.186   [new form 6.61–form 6.63]

8.4   Replacement of exempt property

8.4.1   Where property is excluded from the bankruptcy by s. 283(2) (ie tools of trade, household effects) and it appears to the trustee that its

value exceeds the cost of a reasonable replacement the trustee may
by notice claim the exempt property.
s. 308(1)

8.4.2   Upon service of the notice the property vests in the trustee who has
an application to apply funds in the estate for the purchase of a
reasonable replacement.
s. 308
rr. 6.187 – 6.188

8.5   Income payments orders

8.5.1   The trustee may apply to the court for an income payments order
directing payment to the trustee of part of the income of the
bankrupt.

8.5.2.   The court shall not make an order which would reduce the
bankrupt's income below a sum necessary to meet his reasonable
domestic needs.

8.5.3   The bankrupt may attend the hearing of the application if he gives
notice that he opposes the making of an order or the order proposed
by the trustee. Orders may later be reviewed or discharged.
s. 310
r. 6.189 – 6.193   [forms 6.64 – 6.67]

8.6   Proceedings by mortgagee

8.6.1   A legal or equitable mortgagee may apply to the court for an order
for sale of the bankrupt's land. The court, if satisfied as to the
mortgagee's title, may direct accounts and enquiries to ascertain the
amount due to the mortgagee.
r. 6.197

8.6.2   The court may order any person in possession of the land to deliver
up possession to a purchaser or any other person. Directions may be
given as to the method of sale.
r. 6.198

8.6.3   The sale proceeds shall be applied first, in payment of the expenses
of the trustee occasioned by the application to the court and of the
sale and any taking of accounts and enquiries and secondly, in
payment of the amount due on the mortgage, with any balance going
to the trustee.
r. 6.199

6.6.4   The mortgagee may prove in the bankruptcy for any deficiency but may not disturb any dividend already declared.
r. 6.199(2)

6.7   After-acquired property

6.7.1   Where property is acquired by or devolves upon the bankrupt or where his income is increased he shall within 21 days of his becoming aware of the relevant facts give notice to his trustee.
s. 333(2)
r. 6.200(1)

6.7.2   Having served notice the bankrupt shall not dispose of the property within 42 days.
r. 6.200(2)

6.7.3   If the bankrupt disposes of after-acquired property without giving notice or within the 42 day period the trustee may re-claim it for the estate.
r. 6.200(3)

6.8   Bankrupt's home

6.8.1   The trustee may seek to realise property owned jointly by the bankrupt and spouse or property where the spouse has rights of occupation under the Matrimonal Homes Act 1983.
s. 336(2)

6.8.2   Any application by the trustee in relation to such property shall be made to the court having jurisdiction in relation to the bankruptcy.
s. 336 (3)

6.8.3   The court may make such order as it thinks just and reasonable having regard to:
(1)   interests of the creditors
(2)   conduct of the spouse or former spouse so far as contributing to the bankruptcy
(3)   needs and financial resources of the spouse or former spouse
(4)   needs of any children
(5)   all the circumstances of the case other than the needs of the bankrupt
s. 336(4)

8.8.4   In respect of property owned solely by the bankrupt used as a hom
         for the bankrupt's children under 18 and where there is no spouse o
         none with rights of occupation the bankrupt has a right not to b
         evicted by the trustee without an order of the court. On any suc
         application the court shall have regard to the needs of the children
         s. 337(1), (2) and (5)

8.8.5   Where application is made by the trustee after the expiration of on
         year from the vesting of the estate in the trustee the court sha
         assume that the interests of the creditors outweigh all other consid
         erations.
         s. 337(6)

8.8.6   The effect of these provisions is that in the majority of cases th
         bankrupt's family will be unable to oppose a sale of the home by th
         trustee after one year.

8.9   Transactions at an undervalue

If within the 5 years ending with the day the bankruptcy petition i
presented the bankrupt has:
(1)   made any gift or entered into a transaction under which h
      received no consideration, or
(2)   entered into a transaction in consideration of marriage, or
(3)   entered into a transaction for a consideration which is signifi
      cantly less than that provided
that trustee may apply to the court to restore the position if th
bankrupt was insolvent at the time of the transaction of became so a
a result of it.
ss. 339, 341, 342

8.10   Preferences

The trustee may apply to the court to recover preferences given b
the bankrupt to any person during the 6 months prior to presenta
tion of the petition or to an associate of the bankrupt during the
years prior to presentation of the petition if the bankrupt wa
insolvent at the time or became so as a result of the transaction.
ss. 340 – 342

8.11   Extortionate credit transactions

The trustee may apply to the court to vary or set aside any credi
transactions entered into by the bankrupt within 3 years of th

commencement of the bankruptcy. A transaction is extortionate if the terms of it required grossly exorbitant payments to be made for credit or it otherwise grossly contravened ordinary principles of fair dealing.
s. 343

8.12   Power of arrest

8.12.1   The court has power to issue a warrant for the arrest of a debtor to whom a bankruptcy petition relates, or a bankrupt, or a discharged bankrupt whose estate is still being administered.
s. 364(1)(a)

8.12.2   The warrant may include power to seize any books, papers, records, money or goods in the possession of the arrested person.
s. 364(1)(b)

8.12.3   The court may exercise these powers if at any time after the presentation of a bankruptcy petition it appears that the debtor bankrupt is absconding, removing his goods, or destroying records with a view to defeating the claims of his creditors. The powers may also be exercised when any person fails to attend any examination ordered by the court.
s. 364(2)
rr. 7.19–7.25   [forms 7.6–7.8, new form 7.9, forms 7.10, 7.12, 7.13]

8.13   Seizure of property

8.13.1   After the making of a bankruptcy order the official receiver or trustee may apply to the court for the issue of a warrant for the seizure of any property of the bankrupt. Any person executing such warrant may break open any premises where such property is believed to be.
s. 365(1) and (2)

8.13.2   If the court is satisfied that any property of the bankrupt or records relating to his affairs are concealed in any premises not belonging to the bankrupt it may issue a warrant authorising a constable or prescribed officer of the court to search those premises.
s. 365(3) and (4)
r. 7.25   [forms 7.12, 7.13]

8.14   Enquiry into bankrupt's dealings and property

8.14.1 After a bankruptcy order has been made the official receiver or
trustee may apply for the court to summon before it:
(1) the bankrupt, his spouse or former spouse
(2) any person believed to have property of the bankrupt or to be
indebted to him
(3) any person able to give information about the bankrupt, his
dealings, affairs or property
s. 366   [form 9.1]

8.14.2 If the court is satisfied that any person summoned has property of
the bankrupt or is indebted to him it may order the property to be
delivered or the debt paid.
ss. 367
rr. 9.1 – 9.6

8.15   Re-direction of mail

After the making of a bankruptcy order the official receiver or
trustee may apply to the court for any postal packet addressed to the
bankrupt to be delivered to the official receiver or trustee. Any order
must be for a specified period not exceeding 3 months and may be
applied for from time to time. 'Postal packet' includes all letters,
postcards, parcels and telegrams.
s. 371   [form 6.80]

9. Court Applications

Contents

9.0 Introduction

This chapter gives some general guidance on court applications and procedures in administration, winding up and bankruptcy.

9.1 General applications to the court

9.1.1 An 'originating application' is an application to the court other than in pending proceedings before the court. An 'ordinary application' means any other application.

r. 7.2   [form 7.1 or 7.2]

9.1.2 Applications must be in writing and state the names of the parties, the relief sought, the names and addresses of the persons to be served or that no person is to be served and the applicant's address for service.

r. 7.3

9.1.3 An originating application shall set out the grounds on which the relief sought is applied for.

r. 7.3

9.1.4   The application must be signed by the applicant or his solicitor.
         r. 7.3(3)

9.1.5   The application shall be filed in court with one copy and a number o
         additional copies equal to the number of persons who are to be
         served with it.
         r. 7.4

9.1.6   Unless otherwise provided by the Act or the Rules an application
         must be served at least 14 days before the date fixed for the hearing.
         The court has a general power to abridge time limits in cases of
         urgency.
         r. 7.4(5) and (6)

9.1.7   Applications will usually be made to the registrar in the first
         instance.
         r. 7.6

9.2   Affidavits and reports

9.2.1   Evidence may be given by affidavit unless the Rules otherwise
         provide or the court otherwise directs. The court may order
         cross-examination of any person making an affidavit.
         rr. 7.7, 7.8

9.2.2   A report may be filed instead of an affidavit:
         (1) in any case by the official receiver, or
         (2) unless the application involves other parties, by:
              (a) an administrator, a liquidator or trustee in bankruptcy
              (b) a provisional liquidator or interim receiver,
              (c) a special manager, or
              (d) an insolvency practioner appointed under s. 273(2)
         r. 7.9

9.3   Adjournment of hearings and directions

9.3.1   The court may adjourn any hearing on such terms, if any, as it sees
         fit.
         r. 7.10(1)

9.3.2   The court may give directions as to:
         (1) service of applications
         (2) whether particulars of claim and defence are to be delivered and
              generally as to procedure

(3) the manner in which any evidence is to be given
(4) the matters to be dealt with in evidence
r. 7.10(2)

4 Transfer of proceedings between courts

4.1 Proceedings may be transferred between the High Court and a county court or between county courts. Transfer may only be to a court that has winding-up or bankruptcy jurisdiction.
rr. 7.11–7.15

4.2 Transfer may be ordered by the court of its own motion or by the official receiver or on the application of any person having an interest in the proceedings.
r. 7.11(5)

5 Shorthand writers

In the High Court the judge and, in the county court, the registrar may in writing nominate one or more persons to be official shorthand writers to the court.
r. 7.16(1)   [forms 7.3, 7.4]

5.2 The court may appoint a shorthand writer to take the evidence of a person examined under ss. 133, 236, 290 or 366.
r. 7.16(2)

5.3 The court may direct that the remuneration of the shorthand writer be paid by the party requiring the appointment or out of the estate.
rr. 7.17, r. 7.18

6 Enforcement procedures and warrants

6.1 Orders of the court may be enforced in the same manner as a judgment.

6.2 Warrants under ss. 134(2), 236(5), 364(1), 365(3) and 366(3) are enforced in the High Court by the tipstaff and his assistants, and in the county court by the registrar and the bailiffs.
rr. 7.19–7.25   [forms 7.3, 7.4, 7.6, new form 7.9,
                  forms 7.10, 7.12, 7.13]

7 Court records and returns

7.1 The court shall keep records of all insolvency proceedings with details of all steps taken and decision of the court which shall be

open to inspection by any person. If the registrar is not satisfied as
the propriety of the purpose of the would-be inspector he may refu
to allow inspection. There is a right of appeal to the judge.
rr. 7.27, 7.28

9.7.2   The court shall open and maintain a file in each case and (subject
directions of the registrar) all documents shall be placed on t
relevant file. The file may be inspected by:
(1) the responsible insolvency practitioner
(2) any duly authorised officer of the Department
(3) any creditor
(4) the person to whom the proceedings relate (in company pr
ceedings this includes officers or members), or
(5) any person properly authorised by any of the above
rr. 7.30, 7,3

9.7.3   The court shall give to the Secretary of State brief details of windi
up and bankruptcy proceedings comprising the title, the numb
assigned and the date of any winding up or bankruptcy order.
r. 7.29

9.7.4   Copies of notices published in the Gazette and in newspapers shall l
filed in court.
r. 7.32

9.8   Taxation of costs

9.8.1   Where any costs charges or expenses are payable out of an insolve
estate the insolvency practitioner may agree them or may requi
them to be taxed by the court.
r. 7.34

9.8.2   Where taxation is required a certificate of employment must l
endorsed on the bill and signed by the insolvency practitioner.
r. 7.35(1)

9.8.3   Every person whose costs are to be taxed may be required in writi
to deliver his bill to the taxing officer within 3 months and if he do
not do so and the court does not extend his time his costs are forfei
r. 7.35(3) and (4)

9 Appeals

9.1 The court may rescind or vary any order made in winding-up proceedings.
r. 7.47(1)

9.2 An appeal from a county court or a registrar of the High Court is to a single judge of the High Court. An appeal from a decision of that judge lies, with leave, to the Court of Appeal.
r. 7.47(2) and (3)

9.3 Any application to rescind a winding-up order shall be made within 7 days.
r. 7.47(4)

9.4 An appeal against a decision of the Secretary of State or the official receiver shall be brought within 28 days of notification of the decision.
r. 7.50

IO. Proxies and Representation of Companies Quorum at Meetings

Contents pag

10.0 Introduction

A proxy is an authority given by the principal to the proxy holder t attend a meeting of creditors, company or contributories and spea and vote as his representative. Principal will specify proxy holder (o alternative as proxy holder) by name. Proxy may be given t chairman of meeting or to official receiver if compulsory liquidatio or bankruptcy. Proxy may authorise holder to vote in accordanc with principal's determination (special proxy) or at discretion c holder (general proxy) and may authorise or require holder t propose resolutions.

The prescribed proxy forms are:

8.1 Company or individual voluntary arrangements
8.2 Administration
8.3 Administrative receivership
8.4 Winding up by the court or bankruptcy
8.5 Members' or creditors' voluntary winding up

10.1 Proxy forms

10.1.1 Proxy form is sent out with notice of meeting to be completed an signed by principal, or person authorised by him stating the natur of his authority. Proxy form as sent or in substantially similar form only may be used at meeting.

r. 8.2   [forms 8.1–8.5]

10.1.2 A proxy for a particular meeting may be used at an adjournment. Where official receiver holds proxy he may delegate that authority to deputy, another official receiver or in writing to other officer of the Department.

r. 8.3(2)

10.1.3 Where insolvency practitioner holds proxies to be used by him as chairman, if some other person acts as chairman he may use those proxies. In the absence of specific directions in the proxy, the holder has a discretion as to how to vote.

r. 8.3(3)–(6)*

10.1.4 Proxies used for voting are retained by chairman who must forthwith after meeting deliver them to responsible insolvency practitioner (if not himself).

r. 8.4

10.2 Right to inspect

10.2.1 Responsible insolvency practitioner must allow inspection of proxies lodged with him at all reasonable times on any business day by:
   (1) the creditors (in case of creditors' meeting) being:
        (a) creditors who have proved their debts in a liquidation or bankruptcy
        (b) in other cases, persons who have made written claim to be creditors
   (2) members or contributories (as appropriate meeting)

r. 8.5(1) and (2)

10.2.2 Any person attending meeting may inspect proxies' proofs and associated documents immediately before or during meeting.

r. 8.5(4)*

10.3 Financial interest of proxy holder

Proxy holder (including chairman) must not vote in favour of any resolution which would directly or indirectly place him or any associate of his in a position to receive any remuneration from the insolvent estate, unless proxy specifically directs him to vote that way.

r. 8.6

10.4   Company representation

Where a person not holding a proxy is authorised by resolution to represent a corporation at a meeting, he must produce to the chairman a copy of the duly executed and sealed resolution (under s. 375 Companies Act 1985) giving him such authority.
r. 8.7*

10.5   Lodging

10.5.1   Proxy forms (and proofs to debt) must be lodged at place and by time specified in notice (but final time must not be earlier than 12 am on business day preceeding meeting). Chairman may allow creditor to vote, notwithstanding failure to lodge proof, if satisfied that failure due to circumstances beyond creditors control.
rr. 4.67, 4.68

10.5.2   an individual creditor may, of course, attend and vote at a meeting in person, without lodging a proxy.

10.6   Quorum at meetings of creditors and contributories

10.6.1   Any meeting in insolvency proceedings is competent to act if a quorum is present.
r. 12.4A*

10.6.2   Quorum is:
(1)   for creditors' meeting at least one creditor entitled to vote;
(2)   for contributories' meeting at least two entitled to vote, or all of them if their number does not exceed two.
r. 12.4A(2)*

10.6.3   If rule is satisfied by attendance of chairman alone or with one other and if others may be entitled to vote start of meeting must be delayed for at least 15 minutes.
r. 12.4A(4)*

II.   Dividends

Contents

11.0   Introduction

This chapter deals with the method of distribution of the insolvent estate which is by way of payment of dividends whenever sufficient funds are in hand for that purpose. Before paying any dividend the insolvency practitioner must be satisfied that he will retain sufficient funds to meet the expenses of his administration including his own remuneration. Where creditors have proved for future debts the Rules provide a formula for the calculation of dividends payable before the debt is due.

11.1   Notice of intended dividend

11.1.1   Before declaring a dividend the insolvency practitioner gives notice of his intention to all creditors whose addresses are known who have not proved their debts. The notice specifies the last date for proving which shall be not less than 21 days from the date of the notice. Before declaring a first dividend unless creditors have previously been invited by public advertisement to prove their debts, notice of the intended dividend shall be given by that means.
r. 11.2(1)* and (2)*   [No prescribed form]

11.1.2   The notice states the intention to declare either an interim or final dividend within 4 months of the last date for proving.
r. 11.2(3)

133

11.2   Final admission/rejection of proofs

11.2.1   Within 7 days of the last day for proving, the insolvency practitioner
         shall deal with every creditor's proof by admitting or rejecting it in
         whole or in part. He is not obliged to deal with late proofs, but may
         do so.
         r. 11.3

11.2.2   If a proof is rejected and the creditor appeals to the court the
         insolvency practitioner may postpone or cancel the dividend.
         r. 11.4

11.3   Declaration of dividend

         Notice of the dividend is given to all creditors who have proved their
         debts. The notice gives particulars of all realisations, fees paid and
         funds retained as well as the total amount to be distributed and the
         rate of dividend.
         r. 11.6   [No prescribed form]

11.4   Notice of no dividend

         If the insolvency practitioner gives notice to creditors that he is
         unable to declare any dividend or any further dividend the notice
         shall state either that no funds have been realised or that they have
         already been distributed or used for the expenses of the adminis-
         tration.
         r. 11.7   [No prescribed form]

11.5   Alteration of proof

11.5.1   If a creditor's proof is increased after payment of a dividend he
         cannot disturb the distribution but he is entitled to be paid any
         dividends he has failed to receive before further dividends are paid.
         r. 11.8(1) and (2)

11.5.2   If after a proof is admitted it is withdrawn, expunged or reduced the
         creditor shall repay any sum overpaid by way of dividend.
         r. 11.8(3)

11.6   Secured creditors

         If the security is revalued similar provisions apply to those applicable
         where proofs are increased or reduced.
         r. 11.9

12. Disqualification Provisions

12.0   Introduction

The provisions of the Insolvency Act 1985 and Companies Act 1985 relating to directors' disqualification are consolidated in the Company Directors Disqualification Act 1986 to which this chapter primarily refers.

Directors and shadow directors of insolvent (and solvent) companies may now be subject to disqualification for up to 15 years and/or receive fines in respect of various offences, the measure of the penalty depending on the seriousness of the offence and the directors' culpability.

Directors and other persons may also incur personal liability in certain circumstances mentioned in the Companies Directors Disqualification Act 1986 and also in the Insolvency Act 1986, and may in addition be disqualified.

It is anticipated that the greatest number of disqualification orders will be made on the application of the Department of Trade and Industry under s. 6 of CDDA 1986 (disqualification for unfitness) pursuant to reports (inter alia on conduct) which must now be submitted by the official receiver or insolvency practitioner in office as liquidator, administrator or administrative receiver within 6 months of appointment.

It is anticipated, in s. 18 of CDDA 1986, that a register of disqualification orders will be maintained by the DTI.

12.1 Effect of disqualification

12.1.1 Court may (and under CDDA 1986, s. 6 shall) make disqualification order that person shall not, without leave of court:
(1) be a company director
(2) be a liquidator or administrator
(3) be a receiver or manager of company's property
(4) in any way, directly or indirectly, be involved in promotion, formation or management of a company
for the specified period.

12.1.2 Person may also be criminally liable in respect of those matters. CDDA 1986, s. 1

12.2 General misconduct in relation to companies

12.2.1 Court may make disqualification order where person convicted of indictable offence (on indictment or summarily) in connection with promotion, formation, management, or liquidation of company or receivership or management of company's property.

12.2.2 Jurisdiction:
(1) court having jurisdiction to wind up (that company)
(2) court of conviction (in case of summary conviction may be any magistrates' court in same petty sessions area)

12.2.3 Maximum disqualification:
(1) magistrates' court: 5 years
(2) other court: 15 years
CDDA 1986, s. 2

12.3 Persistent breaches of companies legislation

12.3.1 Court may made disqualification order against person who appears to be in persistent default of his duty to make returns, deliver accounts, send notices etc to registrar of companies. 'Persistent breach' may, inter alia, be proved if 3 or more default orders or convictions in 5 years before application.

12.3.2 Jurisdiction: court having jurisdiction to wind up (that company).

12.3.3 Maximum disqualification: 5 years.

12.3.4 There is similar provision for magistrates' court to make disqualification order following summary conviction for relevant offence.
CDDA 1986, ss. 3,5

12.4 Fraud and other offences in winding up

12.4.1 Court may make disqualification order against person if, in course of winding up, it appears that he:
(1) is guilty of fraudulent trading (whether convicted or not),or
(2) is otherwise guilty, while officer (including shadow director), liquidator or receiver/manager, of fraud or any breach of duty in such capacity

12.4.2 Jurisdiction: court having jurisdiction to wind up.

12.4.3 Maximum disqualification: 15 years.
CDDA 1986, s. 4

12.5 Unfitness

12.5.1 Court must make disqualification order against person if satisfied:
(1) he is or has been director (including shadow director) or company which became insolvent while he was a director or subsequently, and
(2) his conduct as a director of that company makes him unfit to be concerned in the management of another company.

12.5.2. 'Becomes insolvent' means goes into insolvent liquidation, administration or administrative receivership. 'Conduct' means connected with or arising out of the insolvency.

12.5.3 Jurisdiction:
(1) if compulsory liquidation : the winding up court
(2) if voluntary liquidation : any court having jurisdiction to wind up
(3) if in administration : court which made order
(4) if any other case : the High Court.

12.5.4 Minimum disqualification : 2 years
Maximum disqualification : 15 years

12.5.5   Application by DTI through the Secretary of State (official receiver in compulsory liquidation) within 2 years of date company became insolvent, except with leave of court.

Reporting provisions

12.5.6   Every "office holder" (official receiver, liquidator, administrator or adminstrative receiver) submits to DTI within 6 months of appointment, a report on all directors and shadow directors of insolvent company. Office holder can look back 3 years, or more if misconduct occurred during that time. Office holder has duty to report if it appears that 12.4.1 above applies. Office holder must provide relevant information or documentation to Secretary of State (or official receiver) if required.
CDDA 1986, s. 6, 7

Determining unfitness

12.5.7   Matters taken into account whether or not a company is insolvent (extent of directors responsibility in circumstances):
   (1)   misfeasance, or breach of fiduciary duty or other duty
   (2)   misapplication, retention or failure to account for company money or property
   (3)   fraudulent transactions at an undervalue
   (4)   technical breaches of the Companies Act 1985 including the requirements for keeping proper accounting records, keeping the register of directors and secretaries and members up-to-date, filing annual returns and registration of charges
   (5)   failure to prepare annual accounts or have them approved or filed

12.5.8   Matters taken into account where company has become insolvent (extent of directors' responsibility in circumstances):
   (1)   causes of insolvency
   (2)   failure to supply goods or services already paid for, in full or part
   (3)   preference of a creditor or transaction at an undervalue or disposition after commencement of winding up
   (4)   failure to call creditors' meeting, attend meeting and/or produce statement of affairs in creditors voluntary liquidation
   (5)   failure to give information to or co-operate with administrator, administrative receiver or official receiver or liquidator in compulsory winding up
   (6)   failure to deliver up company property
CDDA 1986, Sched 1, Parts I and II

12.6 Participation in fraudulent or wrongful trading

Where court makes declaration under Insolvency Act 1986, s. 213 (fraudulent trading) or s. 214 (wrongful trading) that person is liable to contribute to company's assets, court may also make disqualification order. Maximum disqualification 15 years.
CDDA 1986, s. 10

12.7 Undischarged bankrupts

It is an offence for a person who is an undischarged bankrupt to act as director or be directly or indirectly concerned with promotion, formation or management of a company (except with leave of court by which the person was judged bankrupt, having given notice of application to official receiver who may oppose such application in the public interest).

There is analogous provision where a court revokes an administration order under Part VI of the County Courts Act 1984.
CDDA 1986, ss.11, 12

12.8 Consequences of contravention of a disqualification order, or under 12.7 above

12.8.1 On indictment: maximum 2 years imprisonment or a fine or both
Summary: maximum 6 months imprisonment or a fine or both

12.8.2 A company guilty of such offence and any culpable officer of such company faces similar penalties.
CDDA 1986, ss. 13, 14

12.9 Personal liability

12.9.1 A person is personally liable, jointly and severally with the company and any other such person(s) for any debts and liabilities incurred during such time that:
  (1) he is directly or indirectly involved in the management of a company while disqualified or an undischarged bankrupt, or
  (2) being so involved in the management of a company, he knowingly acts or is willing to act on the instructions of such a person (without leave of the court); once he has acted on the instructions of such person, he is presumed willing to continue to act

12.9.2   Other circumstances where directors or others can incur personal liability:

(1)   fraudulent trading
(2)   wrongful trading
(3)   used company's assets for his own personal benefit
(4)   committed a breach of fiduciary duty
(5)   borrowed company money
(6)   transferred company assets at an undervalue to self or connected person
(7)   misfeasance.
(8)   prohibited re-use of company name
(See generally Chapter X of the Insolvency Act 1986.)
CDDA 1986, s. 15

12.10   Applications for orders

Applicant seeking the making of an order under 12.2 – 12.4 above must give 10 days' notice to respondent who may appear and give evidence or call witnesses.

Applicant may be:

(1)   Secretary of State (DTI) or official receiver
(2)   liquidator
(3)   past or present member or creditor of company in question
CDDA 1986, s. 16

13. Insolvent Partnerships

Contents *page*

13.0 Introduction

The Insolvent Partnerships Order 1986 (IPO) provides a new remedy for a creditor of a partnership. The creditor can bring proceedings for the winding up of a partnership and for the bankruptcy or winding up of two or more of its insolvent members.

13.0.1 A creditor may still present a bankruptcy petition against any individual members of a partnership or a winding up petition against any corporate members. Alternatively a creditor may present a petition for the winding up of an insolvent partnership as an unregistered company under Part V of the Act, which applies subject to certain modifications. Such a petition may now be presented regardless of the number of members of the partnership.

13.0.2 Creditors will generally petition for the winding up of an insolvent partnership and for the bankruptcy or winding up of its individual members, as that would appear to be the only certain way of ensuring a proper distribution of all available assets.

13.0.3 Provision is also made for the partners to be included within the disqualification provisions of the Company Directors Disqualification Act 1986 in relation to unfitness. These provisions may be used to obtain a lengthier period of disqualification than the three year span of a first bankruptcy.

13.0.4 Provision is made for the winding up of the partnership by the members themselves including corporate members.

13.0.5 Bankruptcy petitions may no longer be presented against the partnership or against the individual partners in the name of the partnership.

13.0.6   The IPO provides for a statutory demand by a member of a partnership as a preliminary to a winding up petition against the partnership presented by that member for sums due.

[form 2 IPO]

13.0.7   A liquidator or trustee of an insolvent member may also petition for the winding up of the partnership.

[form 1 IPO]

13.1   Winding up of corporate partners and bankruptcy of individual partners in conjunction with the winding up of the partnership

13.1.1   Creditor serves statutory demand if owed £750 or more.
Schedule 2 IPO   [form 3 IPO]

This demand is addressed to the partnership and if bankruptcy or winding up (as appropriate) of members of partnership is required the demand must state on whom demands will also be served. The demand must also be served on those members.

13.1.2   If payment is not forthcoming within 21 days, creditor may present petitions to wind up partnership in conjunction with petitions against members.

[form 4 IPO]

13.1.3   Petitions against members will be for winding up for any corporate member;

[form 6 IPO]

and for bankruptcy if individual members.

[form 7 IPO]

13.1.4   Petitions should be presented together and only one deposit (currently £240) will be payable.

13.1.5   Creditor advertises petition against partnership and also against any corporate members only.

[form 5 IPO]

13.1.6   Otherwise procedure is as for petitions in bankruptcy and for compulsory winding up.

13.2   Voluntary arrangements

13.2.1   The provisions of the Act relating to company voluntary arrangements apply to corporate members and those relating to individual voluntary arrangements apply to individuals.
Article 11 IPO

8.3   Petition by individual members of insolvent partnership

8.3.1   Where all the partners of an insolvent partnership are individuals a single bankruptcy petition may be presented by them to the court.
Part 4 IPO   [form 8 IPO]

8.3.2   The petition must contain a request that the trustee shall wind up the partnership business and administer the property of the partnership.

8.3.3   All partners must concur in presentation of the petition and an affidavit to that effect must be sworn by the partner who signs the petition.

[no prescribed form]

8.3.4   The only ground for this type of petition is inability to pay debts.

Appendix I
Categories of Preferential Debts

Schedule 6 to the Insolvency Act 1986 contains a list of preferential debts applicable in insolvency of both companies and individuals. Section 387 defines the relevant date as follows:

Relevant date'

For the purposes of s.4 in Part I of the Insolvency Act (meetings to consider company voluntary arrangement), the relevant date in relation to a company which is not being wound up is:

a) where an administration order is in force in relation to the company, the date of the making of that order, and

b) where no such order has been made, the date of the approval of the voluntary arrangement

In relation to a company which is being wound up, the following applies:

a) if the winding up is by the court, and the winding-up order was made immediately upon the discharge of an administration order, the relevant date is the date of the making of the administration order;

b) if the case does not fall within paragraph (a) and the company :
   (i)   is being wound up by the court, and
   (ii) had not commenced to be wound up voluntarily before the date of the making of the winding-up order,

the relevant date is the date of the appointment (or first appointment) of a provisional liquidator or, if no such appointment has been made, the date of the winding up order;

c) if the case does not fall within either paragraph (a) or (b), the relevant date is the date of the passing of the resolution for the winding up of the company.

In relation to a company in receivership (where s.40 or, as the case may be, s.59 applies), the relevant date is that of the appointment of the receiver by the debenture holders.

For the purposes of s.258 in Part VIII of the Insolvency Act (individual voluntary arrangements), the relevant date is, in relation to a debtor who is not an undischarged bankrupt, the date of the interim order made under s.252 with respect to his proposal.

In relation to a bankrupt, the following applies:
(a) where at the time the bankruptcy order was made there was an interim
     receiver appointed under s.286, the relevant date is the date on which
     the interim receiver was first appointed after the presentation of the
     bankruptcy petition;
(b) otherwise, the relevant date is the date of the making of the bankruptcy
     order.

Category 1: Debts due to Inland Revenue

(1) Sums due at the relevant date from the debtor on account of deductions
     of income tax from emoluments paid during the period of 12 months
     next before that date.
(2) Sums due at the relevant date from the debtor in respect of such
     deductions as are required to be made by the debtor for that period
     under s.69 of the Finance (No.2) Act 1975 (sub-contractors in the
     construction industry).

Category 2: Debts due to Customs and Excise

(3) Any value added tax which is referable to the period of 6 months next
     before the relevant date.
For the purposes of this paragraph:
(a) where the whole of the prescribed accounting period to which any value
     added tax is attributable falls within the 6 months period, the whole
     amount of that tax is referable to that period; and
(b) in any other case the amount of any value added tax which is referable to
     the 6 month period is the proportion of the tax which is equal to such
     proportion (if any) of the accounting reference period in question as falls
     within the 6 month period;
     and in sub-paragraph (a) "prescribed" means prescribed by regulations
     under the Value Added Tax Act 1983.
(4) The amount of any car tax which is due at the relevant date from the
     debtor and which became due within a period of 12 months next before
     that date.
(5) Any amount which is due:
     (a) by way of general betting duty or bingo duty, or
(b) under s.12(1) of the Betting and Gaming Duties Act 1981 (general
     betting duty and pool betting duty recoverable from agent collecting
     stakes), or
(c) under s.14 of, or Sched. to that Act (gaming licence duty),
     from the debtor at the relevant date and which became due within the
     period of 12 months next before that date.

Category 3: Social security contributions

) All sums which on the relevant date are due from the debtor on account of class 1 or class 2 contributions under the Social Security Act 1975 or the Social Security (Northern Ireland) Act 1975 and which became due from the debtor in the 12 months next before the relevant date.

) All sums which on the relevant date have been assessed on and are due from the debtor on account of class 4 contributions under either of those Acts of 1975, being sums which:
  (a) are due to the Commissioners of Inland Revenue (rather than to the Secretary of State or a Northern Ireland department), and
  (b) are assessed on the debtor up to 5 April next before the relevant date, but not exceeding, in the whole, any one year's assessment.

Category 4: Contributions to occupational pension schemes etc

) Any sum which is owed by the debtor and is a sum to which Sched 3 to the Social Security Pensions Act 1975 applies (contributions to occupational pension schemes and state scheme premiums).

Category 5: Remuneration, etc, of employees

) So much of any amount which:
  (a) is owed by the debtor to a person who is or has been an employee of the debtor, and
  (b) is payable by way of remuneration in respect of the whole or any part of the period of 4 months next before the relevant date,
  as does not exceed so much as may be prescribed by order made by the Secretary of State.

0) An amount owed by way of accrued holiday remuneration, in respect of any period of employment before the relevant date, to a person whose employment by the debtor has been terminated, whether before, on or after that date.

1) So much of any sum owed in respect of money advanced for the purpose as has been applied for the payment of a debt which, if it had not been paid, would have been a debt falling within paragraph 9 or 10.

2) So much of any amount which:
  (a) is ordered (whether before or after the relevant date) to be paid by the debtor under the Reserve Forces (Safeguard of Employment) Act 1985, and
  (b) is so ordered in respect of a default made by the debtor before that date in the discharge of his obligations under that Act,
     as does not exceed such amount as may be prescribed by order made by the Secretary of State.

Appendix II
Powers of Administrator or Administrative Receiver

Sections 14 and 42 of, and Sched 1 to, the Insolvency Act 1986 empower an administrator or administrative receiver to:

(1) take possession of, collect and get in the property of the company and for that purpose, to take such proceedings as may seem to him expedient

(2) sell or otherwise dispose of the property of the company by public auction or private contract

(3) raise or borrow money and grant security therefor over the property of the company

(4) appoint a solicitor or accountant or other professionally qualified person to assist him in the performance of his functions

(5) bring or defend any action or other legal proceedings in the name and on behalf of the company

(6) refer to arbitration any question affecting the company

(7) effect and maintain insurances in respect of the business and property of the company

(8) use the company's seal

(9) do all acts and to execute in the name and on behalf of the company any deed, receipt or other document

(10) draw, accept, make and endorse any bill of exchange or promissory note in the name and on behalf of the company

(11) appoint any agent to do any business which he is unable to do himself or which can more conveniently be done by an agent and power to employ and dismiss employees

(12) do all things (including the carrying out of works) as may be necessary for the realisation of the property of the company

(13) make any payment which is necessary or incidental to the performance of his functions

(14) carry on the business of the company

(15) establish subsidiaries of the company

(16) transfer to subsidiaries of the company the whole or any part of the business and property of the company

(17) grant or accept a surrender of a lease or tenancy of any of the property of the company, and to take a lease or tenancy of any property required or convenient for the business of the company

(18) make any arrangement or compromise on behalf of the company

148

19) call up any uncalled capital of the company
20) rank and claim in the bankruptcy, insolvency, sequestration or liquidation of any person indebted to the company and to receive dividends,
and to accede to trust deeds for the creditors of any such person
21) present or defend a petition for the winding up of the company
22) change the situation of the company's registered office
23) do all other things incidental to the exercise of the foregoing powers

Appendix III
Powers of Trustee in Bankruptcy

Section 314 of, and Sched 5 to, the Insolvency Act 1986 empower the trustee in bankruptcy to:

Powers Exercisable with Sanction

(1) carry on any business of the bankrupt so far as may be necessary for winding it up beneficially and so far as the trustee is able to do so without contravening any requirement imposed by or under any enactment

(2) bring, institute or defend any action or legal proceedings relating to the property comprised in the bankrupt's estate

(3) accept as the consideration for the sale of any property comprised in the bankrupt's estate a sum of money payable at a future time subject to such stipulations as to security or otherwise as the creditors' committee or the court thinks fit

(4) mortgage or pledge any part of the property comprised in the bankrupt's estate for the purpose of raising money for the payment of his debts

(5) (where any right, option or other power forms part of the bankrupt's estate) make any payments or incur liabilities with a view to obtaining, for the benefit of the creditors, any property which is the subject of the right, option or power

(6) refer to arbitration, or compromise on such terms as may be agreed on, any debts, claims or liabilities subsisting or supposed to subsist between the bankrupt and any person who may have incurred any liability to the bankrupt

(7) make such compromise or other arrangement as may be thought expedient with creditors, or persons claiming to be creditors, in respect of bankruptcy debts

(8) make such compromise or other arrangement as may be thought expedient with respect to any claim arising out of or incidental to the bankrupt's estate made or capable of being made on the trustee by any person or by the trustee on any person

General Powers

(9) sell any part of the property for the time being comprised in the bankrupt's estate, including the goodwill and book debts of any business

(10) give receipts for any money received by him, being receipts which effectually discharge the person paying the money from all responsibility in respect of its application

(11) prove, rank, claim and draw a dividend in respect of such debts due to the bankrupt as are comprised in his estate

(12) exercise in relation to any property comprised in the bankrupt's estate any powers the capacity to exercise which is vested in him under Parts VIII to XI of the Insolvency Act

(13) deal with any property comprised in the estate to which the bankrupt is beneficially entitled as tenant in tail in the same manner as the bankrupt might have dealt with it

Ancillary Powers

(14) For the purposes of, or in connection with, the exercise of any of his powers under Parts VIII to XI of the Insolvency Act, the trustee may, by his official name:
   (a) hold property of every description
   (b) make contracts
   (c) sue and be sued
   (d) enter into engagements binding on himself and, in respect of the bankrupt's estate, on his successors in office
   (e) employ an agent
   (f) execute any power of attorney, deed or other instrument
   and he may do any other act which is necessary or expedient for the purposes of or in connection with the exercise of those powers.